D0713841

Humanics National

PRESCHOOL ASSESSMENT HANDBOOK

A User's Guide to the Humanics National Child Assessment Form— Ages 3 to 6

Derek Whordley, Ph. D. • Rebecca J. Doster

Humanics Limited* Atlanta, Georgia

HUMANICS LIMITED
P.O.Box 7400
Atlanta, Georgia 30309

Revised Edition 1992

Copyright© 1983 by Humanics Limited. All rights reserved.
No part of this book may be reproduced by any means,
nor transmitted, nor translated into a machine language,
without written permission from Humanics Limited.
Library of Congress Card Catalog Number 83-80605

PRINTED IN THE UNITED STATES OF AMERICA
ISBN 0-89334-097-9

Table of Contents

List of Figures and Tables

About the Authors

Dr. Derek Whordley is Professor of Education at the College of Arts and Sciences of Mercer University. His work has included classroom teaching at the early childhood level and the headship of a British infant and junior school. He has made presentations at national and regional conferences of the I.R.A., A.C.E.I., A.S.C.D. and N.C.T.E.

Dr. Whordley completed his undergraduate studies in Britain and graduate work at Michigan State University. With Dr. Jane Caballero, he is the co-author of HUMANICS NATIONAL INFANT-TODDLER ASSESSMENT HANDBOOK and CHILDREN AROUND THE WORLD, published by Humanics Limited.

Rebecca Joyner Doster is actively involved in a variety of voluntary and professional educational activities. Her work has included teaching at the preschool level, Christian education and participation in public school kindergarten programs. She has also conducted seminars for the Girl Scouts of America.

Becky attended Mercer University and the Atlanta College of Art. She is interested in a wide variety of artistic styles and has a local reputation as a color wash artist. Her line drawings illustrate this book.

Becky's continuing interests in the education of young children are reflected in her work with the P.T.A. and her attendance at professional meetings of preschool teachers.

Acknowledgments

The authors wish to acknowledge and express their appreciation to the following who were invaluable in helping put this book together:

Peggi Joyner
Eugenia McGee
Bobbye Raye Kennison
Marie Craig
Kay Sharp
Ann Huff
Betsy Bragg
Burma F. Wright
Frances D. Joyner
Joseph R. Joyner, Sr.
The kindergarten teachers of Lawrenceville Elementary School, Lawrenceville, Georgia
The Gwinnett County, Georgia, Preschool Association
The Georgia Preschool Association

The authors also appreciate the useful contributions and proofreading efforts of Sharan Carpenter, M. Ed.

Introduction

Humanics National Preschool Assessment Handbook is a fundamental introduction to developmental assessment of the preschool child for parents and child development center staff. It is a practical discussion of how to plan and conduct an effective preschool assessment. The handbook describes how to assess the individual child and how to develop an agency or center-wide preschool assessment program. Suggestions for staff and parent training, strategies for parent involvement, a model for implementing the assessment and suggestions for screening for handicapping conditions are outlined.

In addition, *Humanics National Preschool Assessment Handbook* is the user's guide to the *Humanics National Child Assessment Form,** a developmental checklist of skills and behaviors that normally emerge during the three to six year age range. It details specific directions and support materials for using the instrument to develop Individualized Educational Programs, along with guides for planning learning activities for individual children.

This handbook was developed to assist teachers and parents in administering the *H.N.C.A.F.* and using the results most successfully. To derive the greatest benefit from the *H.N.C.A.F.*, it is recommended that you read through the entire manual first. This reading will give you an overview of what to observe and how to interpret and apply findings appropriately.

WHAT YOU WILL FIND IN THE HANDBOOK

In the *Humanics National Child Assessment Form* and this handbook, concepts of child development are integrated with specific behavioral observations. Developmental assessment must be based on an understanding of the processes that are occurring within the child. While almost anyone who is familiar with children can administer the *H.N.C.A.F.*, effective use of the information requires some knowledge of child development.

This handbook is presented in two units. When a person administers the assessment form, he or she should have a sense of the developmental importance of each item. Therefore, Unit I begins with a basic chapter on child development which presents, in plain language, the developmental concepts that underlie the *H.N.C.A.F.*

Chapter One deals with the general topic of child development for children between the ages of three and six years. It explains what you might be expecting from children in the specific areas of Social-Emotional, Language, Cognitive, Motor Skills and Hygiene/Self-Help Development, the areas covered on the *H.N.C.A.F.* This chapter presents the theoretical framework upon which the items on the *H.N.C.A.F.* are built. Additionally, it prepares you to look at each individual child and understand why she might be doing some of the things you see.

Chapter Two then describes preschool assessment and explains how to assess the individual child. It discusses in detail the proper use of the *H.N.C.A.F.*, including who should conduct the assessment, what skills are involved, and how to plan for the assessment. This chapter also reviews the administration of the preschool assessment program. Guidelines to organizing and implementing the assessment procedure and identifying the training which staff and parents need to become involved in the assessment are included. Thus, this handbook is an administrator's manual for preschool assessment, as well as a user's guide to the *H.N.C.A.F.*

Unit II of the handbook is an item by item presentation of the *Humanics National Child Assessment Form.* Chapters Three through Seven relate directly to the items on the assessment form. Each

---

* Available from: Humanics Limited/P.O. Box 7447/Atlanta, Ga. 30309/(404) 874-2176. Please write or call for ordering information.

chapter presents one of the five major areas of child development (Chapter Three: Social-Emotional; Chapter Four: Language; Chapter Five: Cognitive; Chapter Six: Motor Skills; and Chapter Seven: Hygiene/Self-Help) represented on the *H.N.C.A.F.*, and gives an in-depth description of each item contained on the *H.N.C.A.F.*

Specifically, each item is presented with a statement of the developmental significance of that item, a description of how to observe the behavior, suggested learning objectives for a child who does not accomplish the item, and a list of learning activities appropriate to the development of that skill or behavior. These chapters are critical for conducting the assessment and for developing an individualized plan for the child.

Using the child development chapter and the *Developmental Significance* statement presented with each item, even new staff become aware quickly of developmental processes they are observing, rather than simply seeing a series of unrelated behaviors.

Chapter Eight discusses in detail how to use the results you have obtained on the *H.N.C.A.F.* when planning for the child. Insight is offered into the development of the handicapped preschool child and the most beneficial way to use the *H.N.C.A.F.* as a screening tool for special developmental problems. It is particularly useful for alerting you to specific signals that may indicate a handicapping condition. This chapter also contains an example of an Individualized Educational Program developed from the results of a sample *H.N.C.A.F.*, which includes pinpointing long and short range goals and lesson planning.

As mentioned before, we strongly recommend reading this entire handbook before administering the *H.N.C.A.F.* Once you finish reading the handbook, the way is open to observing and assessing young children with a renewed awareness of their individuality.

WHO SHOULD USE THE HANDBOOK AND THE HUMANICS NATIONAL CHILD ASSESSMENT FORM?

This handbook and the *Humanics National Child Assessment Form* are designed for parents with young children and staff of child development programs. Almost anyone familiar with young children can identify the behaviors noted in the instrument. The handbook presents guides to use of the information from the assessment. This format is particularly useful for parents with children at home who want to plan appropriate learning activities for their children.

USING THIS HANDBOOK FOR STAFF AND PARENT TRAINING

In the *Humanics National Preschool Assessment Handbook*, concepts of child development and actual child behavior are integrated into one system of observation and assessment. This model provides an excellent in-service training system for child development center staff, for college and university students in training, and for others who want to understand child development on the practical level.

These materials are particularly effective for parent training. Since the developmental concepts are directly related to behavior parents can observe in their own children, parents quickly identify the concepts of child development and learn to be more skilled observers of their children's behavior.

THE CHILD DEVELOPMENT ASSOCIATE CREDENTIAL

The *Humanics National Preschool Assessment Handbook* is particularly appropriate for candidates seeking the Child Development Associate credential. The functional areas in the CDA require skills in observation and in individualizing the educational program. The *H.N.C.A.F.* provides a specific structure for understanding the developmental progress of the child and for designing specific activities that relate precisely to developmental needs. The CDA candidate will be able to identify developmental processes in the child, as well as discuss what the child can and cannot accomplish.

SCREENING FOR HANDICAPPING CONDITIONS

The *Humanics National Preschool Assessment Handbook* describes how to use the developmental assessment of preschool children as screening for handicapping conditions. Behaviors which signal special problems are described for assessment staff to use as indicators that a particular child may need further evaluation.

SUMMARY

With this handbook and the *Humanics National Child Assessment Form*, we share some of our ideas and experiences with you. We hope you will find the materials useful in your work with your own children and with those in child development centers.

UNIT I

PRESCHOOL ASSESSMENT

Chapter 1

Understanding What You Are Assessing

Understanding basic concepts of the development of preschool age children is necessary to derive the greatest benefit from assessment. It cannot be overemphasized that the application of general concepts of development is most valuable when considered in relationship to the *individual* child. It is both impossible and unrealistic to say, "All three year olds . . ." or "A five year old should be . . . " By recognizing the individuality of each child, we can offer experiences most appropriate to enhancing the particular blend of heredity and environment unique to that child.

The *H.N.C.A.F.* focuses assessment of the child in five major areas of development.

- Social-Emotional
- Language
- Cognitive
- Motor Skills
- Hygiene and Self-Help

There will be children whose strongest area of development is in one of these domains. In addition, while several children may exhibit strength in the same domain, they may have accomplished different skills represented by the *H.N.C.A.F.* items in that section. The intent of the assessment is not to categorize the child, but to characterize and document her achievements.

This chapter on child development offers some basic concepts to guide teachers in understanding the processes represented by the five major areas of early childhood development. It is important to consider each developmental area separately and then in interaction with each other. The child is a product not only of each dimension of maturational development, but also of the way in which they fit together to become the whole individual. The following sections of this chapter discuss social-emotional development, language development, cognitive development, motor development and hygiene and self-help as these dimensions relate to the scales on the *H.N.C.A.F.*

SOCIAL-EMOTIONAL DEVELOPMENT

Between the ages of three and six, the child is very egocentric. She sees herself as the most important person in the world, is extremely sensitive to the criticisms of others, and has difficulty seeing anything she does as "wrong". Those involved in early childhood education must seriously consider this self-centered quality when deciding how best to interact with the young child. Our reactions and attitudes can be very significant in determining how the child feels about herself and her relationship to others.

Your program may be the first formal learning experience for many of the children you serve. This presents a perfect opportunity to offer the child a positive experience that may affect her attitude about school and learning for years to come.

Items 1-18 on the *H.N.C.A.F.* are concerned with social-emotional development. Those items reflecting social development focus on the ability to get along with others, i.e., cooperating, showing social awareness, and building relationships to parents, adults in general, and other children. The items dealing with emotional development are concerned with the child's self-concept development and the ability to express and control feelings.

COOPERATION

To be able to cooperate with others, the child must become less self-centered and begin to understand another person's point of view. In fact, it is not surprising to find the youngest children and those who have had little experience with other children having a difficult time sharing or taking turns. It is important to encourage and even enforce the need to cooperate. Patient, gentle understanding will be required since the child is likely to respond with a sense of frustration until maturity and experience dictate otherwise. Whenever possible, praise the child for sharing or merely participating in an activity with another child. At first, try to keep the length of time the child has to wait for a "turn" to a minimum. As cooperation appears on the child's own initiative, the length of time will be less significant and frustrated responses will begin to disappear.

SOCIAL AWARENESS

Socialization begins at birth. Naming a child, clothing her, and feeding her are all influenced by social customs. Many of the messages we convey to the infant reveal our social expectations. "Give Grandma a kiss", for example, tells the child that this is a desired and socially appropriate behavior.

As the child develops, social responsibilities become internalized and constant reminders become unnecessary. Social awareness is revealed in the child's interactions with other people, as well as in her actions toward taking responsibility for the materials she uses. Social restrictions (e.g., "We do not hit our friends," "We must put our puzzles away when we are finished") become clear to the child early in group experiences. The teacher and parent must remember, though, that in dealing with a child for whom "I" is of supreme importance, acting in socially appropriate ways is a difficult thing to learn. Some of the items on the *H.N.C.A.F.* (#5, 12, 14, 15, 16, for example) are designed to assist us in evaluating how socially aware the child is. Once this is ascertained, we can design activities to encourage the further development of this area of social-emotional growth.

RELATIONSHIP TO OTHERS

Learning to relate to others, adults and children alike, is the primary goal of social development. The process begins in infancy, with the parent(s) being the initial partners in a special relationship. The bond created between parent and child is strong, and parents should be aware that this relationship begins to form the first time they make eye or body contact with the child. It is possible that the potential for significant messages to be transmitted to the baby is available long before any type of identifiable responses from the child are observed. These first interactions and those throughout the period of infancy establish the basis on which trust in interpersonal relationships will grow.

Similarly, the child's first school experiences will serve as a model for future attitudes involving teachers and others in such settings. Therefore, it is important to maintain the type of environment appropriate to this responsibility. Young children often pattern their own behavior after that of the significant adults in their lives. Teachers and parents should be concerned not only with the ways they interact directly with the children, but also with their own behavior as it represents a model to be imitated. Watching children role playing "teacher" (or "parent") is a good way to find out how they perceive adults.

Interacting with adults other than family members may be a relatively new experience for the child. Initially, dependent behavior (e.g., clinging to parent or teacher, requiring a good deal of holding and cuddling, talking reluctantly with adults) should be expected. As the child becomes more accustomed to the surroundings and people in the center, the dependent behavior should diminish.

SELF-CONCEPT

The image a person has of him or herself is termed the self-concept. This image begins developing early in infancy as the parents communicate to the child through such behaviors as eye contact, body contact, tone of voice, verbal exchanges, and facial expressions. The child's feelings of self-worth are greatly influenced by these early transactions. Making these experiences as warm and loving as possible will encourage the child to develop healthy feelings of self-importance. With continued reinforcement, these feelings will blossom as the child grows.

Young children are most likely to develop a positive self-concept in a supportive and consistent environment. Therefore, it is a good idea to speak to the child in a way that communicates that she is important, loved and accepted. For example, a child might be seeking attention at a time when the teacher or parent is occupied with another task. There are several ways to respond to the child, each of which conveys a clear message about attitude. For example, to support the child's positive feelings about herself, the adult could bend down to be on eye-level with the child, look at her directly, perhaps touch a shoulder or put an arm around her, and say, "Susie, I am busy doing something right now, but I know what you need is important too, so I will be with you just as soon as I can." By doing so, the teacher or parent will relay his or her concern about the child's needs while simultaneously encouraging the child's self-control so that she will be able to wait for those needs to be met.

Parents and teachers want to foster the child's positive feelings, but since they will not always be present to offer direction, they must also show the child that, essentially, she is responsible for herself. Setting specific behavior limits for the classroom or home is crucial to the child's sense of well-being. These limits encourage the child to exhibit self-control in situations where the first response might be to act impulsively. Knowing that she can, indeed, be responsible for herself is a significant element of the child's self-concept.

EXPRESSING AND CONTROLLING FEELINGS

Spontaneous display of feelings is characteristic of the very young child. The infant reacts to stimulation by crying, laughing, waving arms, turning the head, etc. Although she is unable to differentiate among feelings, the child can exhibit demonstrative behavior to elicit a response from an attending adult.

As the child matures, it is important to differentiate between "displaying feeling" and "expressing feelings." "Displaying feelings" suggests the infantile expression of spontaneous reactions. For example, the baby cries to signify hunger, pain, or fright, without being able to distinguish which of these sensations is the stimulus. The more mature young child must be encouraged, instead, to "express feelings" by clearly identifying what the feelings are. Labeling these feelings is a first step. Is the child angry? Are there hurt feelings? Is she happy?

When children are discouraged from expressing their true feelings, displays of inappropriate behaviors may follow. A child who does not know how to identify the fact that she is angry or who is discouraged from saying, "I am feeling angry," for example, might throw something to display the anger. Children can display positive feelings inappropriately as well. A child who is unaccustomed to experiencing or expressing happiness may respond by being overly affectionate. Whether positive or negative, children will reveal their feelings in one form or another. Keys to the child's healthy emotional development are the abilities to identify, verbalize, and control the expression of feelings appropriately.

LANGUAGE

The development of language skills parallels the development of thought processes. Where the infant thinks only in mental images, the preschooler thinks in words, which enables her to conceptualize relationships and use reasoning in thinking. Preschool age children are in the process of becoming adept at using language and need ample opportunities to practice and expand their word experiences. By selecting and rejecting words for use in certain contexts, the child gains skill in speaking, and consequently she finds logical thought easier. When a person has to search for the proper words to express ideas, the ideas often become clearer and more meaningful. Therefore, offering the child a wide variety of experiences with new words will broaden her vocabulary and improve both communication and reasoning abilities.

The development of language occurs in two separate but interrelated stages. By discussing language as "receptive" and "expressive," we can more clearly understand how language develops.

RECEPTIVE LANGUAGE

Even before the child is able to speak, she experiences symbolic messages that form the basis of thoughts. Receptive language includes all of the information the child is taking in, whether it is in the form of mental images or words. An infant recognizes the face of her parent or a familiar toy, but she does not yet have a word for the object that she recognizes. As she becomes used to hearing sounds associated with objects, mental images and words begin to go together, and the child becomes open to verbal instruction. She is able to follow simple commands such as, "come here" and "bring me the book."

A child learns language by hearing and not primarily by direct instruction. Adults have many opportunities to use language with and to speak to young children, so that the child's listening and eventually speaking vocabulary will increase rapidly. Receptive language thus develops first, and the ability to use mental representations becomes more sophisticated as the child matures.

EXPRESSIVE LANGUAGE

Expressive language develops at a rapid pace, particularly between the ages 18 months and 4 years, and is the foundation for much of the child's lifetime communications. When the child develops the ability to speak, she becomes able to convey her thoughts and wishes to others, and to exert greater control over her experiences. Where previously the child depended on action as her only mode of expression, she now has added the futher dimension of verbal expression.

The toddler's first words are usually nouns or labeling words, such as "mama", "dada", or "ball". She then progresses to two-word sentences usually utilizing a noun plus a verb or a noun plus an adjective, i. e., "dog bark" or "dog big." Between 18 months and 4 years, children learn the basics of their native tongue, including most grammar rules and a vocabulary of approximately 1,000 words. They can produce grammatically correct sentences, but may not fully comprehend the meaning of the words they use.

Adult guidance is an important part of language development. Rather than correcting a child's attempt at forming sentences, the adult can be helpful by expanding the child's sentence. (Example: Child: "Baby eat"; Adult: "Yes, the baby is eating.") As vocabulary and understanding increase, the child uses her imagination to create stories and play many roles. While observing her at play, take note of the child's conversing quite seriously with dolls, stuffed animals, pets, or any other objects that will "listen."

COGNITIVE DEVELOPMENT

Cognitive development refers to the intellectual growth of an individual. This process begins at birth and progresses through a number of stages until the individual reaches intellectual maturity. Each individual moves through these stages in the same order, but the rate at which each proceeds varies from person to person. Offering a wide variety of stimulating experiences to the child will present the opportunity to see her exercise her cognitive powers to their fullest extent. This practice will encourage the rate of development to proceed to the optimum level potential.

To assess the development of young children, it is necessary to understand the way the child processes the vast amount of information she encounters. Such understanding is not always easy, particularly since mental processing is not something we can see. We can only look at the child's behaviors and try to understand what these behaviors represent.

Aspects of cognitive development represented by the items on the *H.N.C.A.F.* comprise the following processes.

MEMORY

Remembering information means that the child is able to make mental representations of the things she is learning. This function is crucial since it represents the ability to retrieve stored information and apply it to solving problems.

At a very basic level, memory is involved in virtually all aspects of learning. From the time the child shows any type of recognition of her parents or specific objects we can assume that the most elementary roots of memory are beginning to grow. For the infant, these spurts of recognition do not last very long and once the object or person is removed from the child's vision, in the child's mind the object no longer exists. As the child's cognitive processes develop, she becomes able to retain a sense of the significance of objects and people and begins to make connections among them. As this development continues, the child's memory will be able to process increasingly more complex representations which will be used in all facets of cognitive experiences.

IMAGINATION

Using imagination reflects the child's ability to take what she knows in one context and use it in a novel fashion. Encouraging the use of imagination as the child exhibits readiness will foster its development. For example, asking the child to name all possible uses of an item (such as blocks on sticks) entices her to begin using some information she already has learned creatively.

Encouraging the child to use imagination also conveys the message that there is not always one "right" solution to a problem. In fact, the more novel responses the child is able to produce, the more she will be exercising thought processes. As the problems confronted become more difficult, the ability to use imagination in creating solutions will be most valuable.

Imaginative experiences also benefit the child in working through personal problems. Preschool age youngsters are at a stage where pretending about things that trouble them can be most constructive. One might find a child in the housekeeping corner, for example, pretending to be a parent severely reprimanding a child. This behavior might be an indication that she is trying to come to terms with a problem at home.

The attitudes of adults who are in day-to-day contact with children strongly influence how free the youngsters feel to express themselves creatively. Adults should encourage innovative responses to continue this line of development.

THINKING

"Thinking" is a rather general term that refers to the mental processing of information. As an infant in the first stage of cognitive development, the child begins taking in the stimuli around her but is unable to give it meaning. Experiences with the world are gathered through sensory faculties of vision, taste, touch, hearing, and smell. Once the sensory experience ends, the child forgets about it. As development progresses, the child becomes able to take the information she has received through the senses, categorize, classify and remember it, and use it to its fullest advantage.

Be aware that preschool age children are at a stage where they are able to concentrate on only one characteristic of an object at a time. Since visual perceptions are the ones that are the most obvious to the child, the characteristic of an object which is most visually prominent will be the one the child attends to first. For example, if a set of coins is placed before the child in a particular arrangement, she is likely to think that the number of coins has changed if the coins are bunched up or spread out. The child is relying on her perception of how the arrangement "looks." This style of thinking will change as the child matures and becomes able to consider more than one variable at a time.

PROBLEM SOLVING

Solving problems is an aspect of cognitive development that involves all the other areas previously discussed — memory, imagination, and thinking, as well as language. In fact, if we were to try to characterize a child's cognitive development in one simple phrase, "problem solving" would be a good choice. All aspects of life involve facing problems and learning to solve them. The tiny infant who is able to grab the rattle dangling overhead has, in essence, solved a problem. As the child's development proceeds, the problems become more complex and the ability to deal with them becomes more refined.

It is important that we do not underestimate how difficult learning is for the young child. Adults often forget what it feels like to be a youngster and find it hard to identify with their problems. Whenever possible, it is a good idea to look at things from the child's point of view to remind ourselves of how significant her dilemmas are. In actuality, a young child must create the entire world for herself, and we, as adults, can only provide appropriate challenging experiences as guidance. Every new experience involves taking in information, mentally processing it and arriving at a solution.

The cognitive process is a complex one which continues to develop throughout our lives. The better our initial experiences are, the stronger our base for solving problems.

MOTOR SKILLS

The ability to control body movements is a component of the child's development that can substantially influence self-image. The awkward child, for example, is likely to feel self-conscious about her movements and may be reluctant to participate in physical activities. The more coordinated child, on the other hand, will find feelings of adequacy accompanying skill in body control. As the child's motor abilities progress, self-image is affected by the way others respond to newly-developed skills. Their responses, in turn, influence her own evaluation of these abilities. Self-reliance increases with body control and the child's positive self-concept is reinforced accordingly.

Physical growth and the opportunity to exercise the appropriate skills lay the foundation for body control. Infants are born with all the structures necessary for motor control, as well as the ability to control muscles and movement, but physical maturity and experience are required to achieve motor development.

Body growth proceeds rapidly for the very young child. In fact, one of the two most rapid periods of growth occurs just before birth. (The other period is at the beginning of puberty.) Birth to age two is also a time of considerable growth, but age two to four is one of the slowest. We find the periods of more rapid growth accompanied by awkward types of movements, while the slower stages seem to give the child the opportunity to sharpen her skills.

There are two major functional areas characterizing infancy that are preliminary to further developmental progress in motor ability. The first is upright locomotion. The infant progresses from spending the majority of her time lying down to sitting up, and then to standing. Movement from an upright position is necessary to gross motor abilities such as walking, balancing, running, and jumping.

Manipulability, i.e., the ability to reach with the hand, grasp, and manipulate an object, is the second preliminary functional ability. The baby progresses from reaching in the general direction of an object to swiping at the object, to actually grasping it, and finally, manipulating or retrieving it. This skill is prerequisite to such future fine motor abilities as drawing, writing, catching a ball, or holding and using scissors.

GROSS MOTOR SKILLS

Gross motor skills are those involving the large muscles of the body such as muscles in the arms and legs. An infant's first step and a preschooler's first swing with a bat are examples of unpolished displays of gross motor skills.

Up until approximately four years of age, the growth in the muscular system is roughly proportionate to the growth of the rest of the body. After that, the muscles develop at a faster rate so that about seventy-five percent of the child's weight increase during the fifth year can be attributed to muscle development. The large muscles are better developed than the small fine muscles during early childhood. The increased rate of development of the large muscles is greatly responsible for the preschool child being more skillful in activities requiring large movement and balance than those requiring finer coordination.

Body control proceeds from large to smaller muscles. During the preschool period gross motor skills become refined, representing the development of body control. For example, running gets smoother, with acceleration and deceleration becoming easier. Turning corners and stopping are accomplished more easily also. Jumping up and down in place, which is characteristic of the younger child, leads to the abilities to jump from a stool with her feet together, to skip and to hop. Dancing and keeping time to music also reflect a refined degree of gross motor skills.

Balance is a component of gross motor ability that is required for the accomplishment of many of the skills represented on the *H.N.C.A.F.* The child must be able to center her weight to achieve balance and this balance is a necessary factor in mastering body control. Such behaviors as walking on tip toes, jumping from a stool, standing on one foot and walking backwards, all require balance. As balance improves, a sense of self-reliant abandon is reflected in the child's motor behavior.

FINE MOTOR SKILLS

Fine motor skills utilize the small muscles of the body, such as those in the fingers and toes. These skills are more difficult to achieve than those requiring the larger muscles and are generally mastered after gross motor abilities are under control.

The preschooler is continually improving her fine motor skills through maturity and exercise. We find the strokes in drawing better defined and less repetitive as she develops. The figures she copies are more complex and, in fact, she is able to draw a recognizable human figure. Using scissors, tearing paper, stringing beads, and stacking blocks are some more examples of the skills reflecting fine motor capacity.

It is interesting to note that as the child's abilities become more sophisticated, the intentions behind her behaviors change as well. The young child progresses from engaging in an activity merely for the pleasure of being active to participating in an activity where the task is only part of a game or play. For example, as the child's coordination and fine motor ability increases, she moves from simply stacking blocks to using them in dramatic play and to make houses, buildings, tables, chairs, etc. Additionally, we find her drawings going from scribbling to actual attempts to reproduce reality. These skills reflect an advance in motor skill development, as well as a general progression from immature behavior to skilled control of abilities.

HYGIENE AND SELF-HELP DEVELOPMENT

The healthy development of the young child is greatly influenced by the ability to take care of herself. The infant is totally dependent on others to gratify needs and tend to her general welfare. As the child grows, she gradually develops skills which lead to her emergence as an independent individual. Self-reliance is a most desirable trait and the more frequent the opportunities to develop it, the more self-sufficient the child will become. The areas of Hygiene and Self-Help skills represent the components of development reflecting the child's ability to care for personal needs in healthy ways. These skills are crucial to the child's becoming a responsible individual.

HYGIENE

Hygiene skills involve recognizing and attending to physical needs in healthy ways. From infancy, the child is experienced in signaling various needs, although she has been unable to identify them specifically. Crying is the generalized signal of distress the baby uses whenever a need arises. Physical needs such as hunger, thirst, uncomfortable temperature, diaper discomfort, and pain are associated with crying. They are the easiest for the preschooler to recognize and express since she has experienced them since babyhood. The difference now, of course, is that in addition to acknowledging the existence of the needs, she must learn to take responsibility for satisfying them.

The preschool age child is generally eager to take additional responsibility for her own needs. She feels like a "big girl" when given the opportunity, for example, to help with cleaning up, dressing herself, or managing her own bathroom needs. There should be ample opportunities for her to do these things on her own.

In is important at this point for the significant adults in the child's life to examine their own attitude in relation to the child's developing independence. Frequently, adults profess to wanting the child to attend to her own needs, but in practice, they are reluctant to relinquish control. A child who can dress herself, attend to toilet needs, put toys and clothes away, etc., is no longer a baby. She is demonstrating an independence that a parent or teacher may be unwilling to accept.

We must keep in mind that the child's readiness to accept responsibilities and do things for herself must be accompanied by the opportunity to do so. Parents and teachers should prepare themselves to encourage self-sufficiency even if it means having to tolerate some accidents (e.g., in trying to clean up a spill, the child actually makes more of a mess) and confusion (e.g., while trying to put away her clothes, the child pulls the dresser drawer out and everything lands on the floor).

The area of hygiene skill development also includes nutrition and general health. Taking care of physical needs requires knowledge of basic nutrition and its relationship to overall health and well-being. The healthy child is likely to be superior in all aspects of life to a child in poor health, and appreciation of this fact should be conveyed to the child.

The preschool child is likely to take cues from the adults and other children around her. It is important, then, that we set good examples in maintaining our own health standards by, for example, trying new foods and encouraging a well-balanced diet as a routine part of daily living. The child should be offered frequent opportunities to experiment with new foods and learn about their food values. These experiences will serve as the basis for understanding how good nutrition is critical to good health.

SELF-HELP

The development of self-help skills means that the child is able to accept responsibility for her actions and to take care of herself in generally safe and accepted ways. These skills go beyond caring for physical and health needs to the more general acceptance of responsibility for overall behavior. Infants and toddler react without regard for the possible results or consequences. Awareness of responsibility accompanying behavior is an indication of developmental maturity. When a child is able to recognize that the things she does are associated with consequences, she is on her way to becoming independent. She is able to see beyond the immediacy of a particular action and can evaluate the result of her behavior.

As mentioned in the previous section, adults serve as models for the child. Our behavior will be imitated and, therefore, we must be careful to "practice what we preach." If we admonish the child to clean up after herself, we must be certain to do the same. If we solicit the child's assistance in fulfilling our responsibilities, we should be prepared to be asked for help in return.

Setting rules and limits in the classroom or home is an integral part of fostering the development of the child's ability to recognize and accept responsibility. Expectations must be clearly stated so there is no ambiguity in what the child is to do. Enforcing these limits consistently will give the child a feeling of security as she engages in the difficult process of taking responsibility for her own actions.

Taking care of herself and satisfying her own needs can greatly influence the child's self-concept. Something as simple as being able to recite her address and phone number can be a great source of pride for the child, and we must reinforce these accomplishments whenever possible. Self-reliant behavior is necessary if the child is to develop the capability to manage her life, and the development of self-help skills is a necessary component to self-sufficiency.

SUMMARY

Items on the *Humanics National Child Assessment Form* identify behaviors that indicate progress in the five developmental areas presented above. To conduct meaningful assessment, the observer must be aware that the behavior itself is significant primarily as an index of the developmental process. Planning for the child must be based on the individual developmental level, and items on the *H.N.C.A.F.* provide a system for understanding where the child is functioning.

Chapter 2

How to Use The Humanics National Child Assessment Form

The *Humanics National Child Assessment Form (H.N.C.A.F.)* is a checklist of observable skills and behaviors a child is likely to develop during the ages three to six years. It is a guide for teachers and parents to understanding child development.

Assessment is an integral part of the teaching process and results may be used as a basis for individualized instruction. The *H.N.C.A.F.* helps parents and teachers identify skills and behaviors that individual children have already developed, and plan learning experiences which encourage continued growth. The checklist is a guide to systematic observation of important facets of development. Since children develop at their own rate and the individual differences between children are what make each special, this checklist is presented as a tool for working with the child and *not* as a test.

A key to using the instrument is understanding that young children best demonstrate what they know and what they can do by their behavior. One cannot rely on a three year old to write something to show what he knows, or count on him to describe things accurately. The best one can do is watch very carefully to see which behaviors are occurring, note their frequency, and take these as indications of developmental progress. Of course, one must know what to look for to be able to interpret what is seen meaningfully. The *H.N.C.A.F.* was developed to structure observation of specific skills and behaviors that represent various levels of growth.

CONTENT OF THE HUMANICS NATIONAL CHILD ASSESSMENT FORM

The *Humanics National Child Assessment Form* is a checklist of behaviors characteristic of children ages three to six years. As has been stated, broad developmental areas are represented on the five behavior scales of the instrument:

- Social-Emotional
- Language
- Cognitive
- Motor Skills
- Hygiene and Self-Help

Each scale has eighteen items.

Items on the five scales of the assessment form are arranged in a generally progressive sequence. Task and skill mastery expected at an earlier age are presented at the beginning of each scale and are followed by increasingly difficult tasks at the end of the scale. Each multiple-item scale spans the age range of three to six years. For example, on the cognitive scale, item #37 "Visually Discriminates Between Colors" is a less difficult task, representing a more quickly developed skill (nearer the 3.5 year range), than is item 47 "Understands Relative Qualities" (nearer 4.5-5.0 year age range).

The instrument is designed to record information from four separate assessments of the child. This arrangement is particularly suited for parental use since parents are able to monitor development over several years. Interested parents should learn to complete the assessments on their own. In child development programs, the scales allow for a progressive record of the child's development. The choice of how often to administer the assessment is left to the staff, but a formal assessment at least twice a year is recommended.

Chapters Three through Seven of the handbook present an item-by-item discussion of the developmental items in the *H.N.C.A.F.* At the top of each page is a box containing the item to be discussed, reprinted exactly as it appears on the *H.N.C.A.F.* Below that is a paragraph labeled *Developmental Significance*. This statement explains the importance of the item in developmental terms. Those administering the assessment should use those statements to be alert to the developmental processes that are occurring within the child.

The statement of *Developmental Significance* is followed by a paragraph labeled *Task Description*. This paragraph is an explanation of what behaviors you should look for in deciding whether the child is able to accomplish the task. It specifies any materials that might be required to evaluate the item and the types of situations in which the existence of the skill is likely to appear.

After reading the statement of *Developmental Significance* and the *Task Description*, you will need to decide whether the behavior exists for each child. Record the evaluations on the *Humanics National Child Assessment Form* itself (NOT the handbook). If the characteristic is not present or the behavior does not occur, leave everything blank in the columns next to the item. If the characteristic or behavior is present sometimes, but is not a consistent part of the child's behavior pattern, put a check in the "Occurs Occasionally" column next to the appropriate item. This designation means that the behavior has appeared but is not firmly mastered or developed.

Take item #37, "Visually Discriminates Between Colors", for example. A child might correctly identify an object as red for you one day and the next he may be unable to do so. You would put a check in the "Occurs Occasionally" column, because, although the identification was demonstrated once correctly, it is not a consistent part of the child's behavior. Those skills checked under the "Occurs Occasionally" column will be the ones to return to after the entire evaluation has been completed. They need to be strengthened.

If the characteristic or behavior has been adequately mastered and developed, and occurs as a normal part of the child's behavior, put a check in the "Occurs Consistently" column. This designation means that your evaluation indicates the child is capable of performing the required task or exhibiting the required behavior at this point in her development.

Space has been provided on the *H.N.C.A.F.* for assessing the child four times during the year. The actual number of assessments done is left to the staff of individual programs. We strongly recommend, however, that each time an assessment is planned, a two-week period be designated as the evaluation period. This period should allow enough time for each child to be assessed and give sufficient time between evaluation periods for interpreting the results and planning appropriate experiences.

Once an evaluation period is completed, the next step is to complete the *Child Development Summary Profile*, found on the back page of the *H.N.C.A.F.*, and to use these results in selecting activities most helpful to the child. In completing the Profile, circle those items that you have checked "occur occasionally" in one color and those checked "occur consistently" in another color.

The Profile will give you a quick visual summary of the child's progress. From there decide which items are more difficult for the child, and then return to the handbook to choose activities to help strengthen these areas. The description of each *H.N.C.A.F.* item in Chapters Three through Seven includes a section labeled *Suggested Activities*. These suggestions are offered to assist in planning an individual educational program for each child. These activities, however, are certainly not the only ones appropriate for aiding in the development of the particular abilities found on the *H.N.C.A.F.* Each teacher and parent is urged to add others. Teacher and parent input is especially important because it is not realistic to expect the same activities to be meaningful to all children.

Individualized planning is based on the patterns of a child's behavior that "occur occasionally" and "occur consistently". A sample profile is presented in Chapter Eight to demonstrate the completed *H.N.C.A.F.* checklist for a child.

WHO SHOULD CONDUCT THE ASSESSMENT?

The *Humanics National Child Assessment Form* was designed in response to the need of parents and child development program staff for a simple but useful assessment and planning tool. Items on the instrument reflect common behavioral indicators which most parents and others associated with young children will recognize. Therefore, most child development center staff, teachers, aides, etc., as well as parents of young children, can readily use the checklist to structure assessment observations and to plan individualized learning experiences for the child. Parent participation is desirable, and parents should be encouraged to come to the center and observe the child in interaction with other children. The parent's observations will be different from the teacher's, and comparison will establish a basis for in-depth discussion of the child and her development. At the same time, parents will learn to develop objectivity in viewing their child.

Figure I presents a sample note to parents informing them of the intended assessment of their child and inviting their participation. Supplementary letters (Figures II and III) may also be sent to parents.

FIGURE I
SAMPLE NOTE TO PARENTS INFORMING THEM OF THE PROGRAM'S INTENTION TO DO A DEVELOPMENTAL ASSESSMENT OF THEIR CHILD.

INTENTION TO CONDUCT DEVELOPMENTAL ASSESSMENT

The (Name of Program) will be conducting a developmental assessment of your child (child's name) along with all other children in our center during the period (date) through (date). This is part of the procedure the center follows in order to plan an individualized educational program for your child.

The *Humanics National Child Assessment Form* will be used to help structure the observation of your child. This instrument focuses on social-emotional development, language development, cognitive development, motor skills, and the development of hygiene and self-help skills. These represent important areas of development for children in the three to six year age range.

You are invited to join the teacher in conducting the assessment observations of your child. We request that you come to the center to observe your child in the activities and in interaction with the other children here. You and the teacher will be able to compare your observations.

Please contact (teacher's name) at (address) or phone (number) to schedule a time to observe your child at the center.

Sincerely,

_____ Center Director

FIGURE II
SUPPLEMENTARY LETTER TO PARENTS I
PARENT CONFERENCE

Dear (Parent's Name),

Assessments and conferences with our parents have been set up for the week of_____.
I would like to meet with you at this time so that we can work together in (child's name)'s
behalf.

Below is a conference date. Please let me know if it is convenient for you by filling out the
attached form and sending it back to school.

Thank you,

_____

Teacher's Signature

****

Dear (Parent's Name),

I have scheduled your conference on (_____date_____) at (___time___).

_____

Teacher's Signature

****

Dear (Teacher's Name),

I have received your note informing me of the date and time of my conference.

I can attend ☐

I cannot attend ☐

I could attend _____
                        (Alternative date and time)

_____

Parent's Signature

FIGURE III
SUPPLEMENTARY LETTER TO PARENTS II
Questionnaire

Dear (Parent's Name),

Please take a moment and answer these questions concerning your child. If you would, bring the questions and answers to our conference.

Thank You,

Teacher's Signature

PRENATAL HISTORY

1. Prematurity?	Yes	No	If yes, give details
2. Prolonged Labor?	Yes	No	If yes, give details
3. Blood incompatibility?	Yes	No	If yes, give details

DEVELOPMENTAL HISTORY

1. Crawling	Early	Normal	Late/Abnormal
2. Walking	Early	Normal	Late/Abnormal
3. Tip-toe walking		Normal	Prolonged
4. Speech	Early	Normal	Late/Abnormal
5. Ambidexterity (after age 7)	Yes	No	
6. Adoption	Yes	No	

PRESENT

1. How does your child feel about school?
2. How well does your child listen when others are speaking? Does your child follow directions at home?
3. Does your child take pride in completing tasks at home?
4. What tasks is your child responsible for at home?
5. How does your child feel about competition?
6. Does your child have friends outside of school friends?
7. Does your child seem to be sensitive to the needs of others?
8. What is your child's usual bedtime?
9. Are you happy with your child's bathroom and eating habits?
10. What does your child like to do after school?
11. How much television does your child watch?
12. Does your child talk to you about his/her day at school?

Typically, in a child development center the child's teacher or aide is responsible for assessing a particular child. Since the *H.N.C.A.F.* is an observation tool and the assessment may extend over a week or two, however, it is possible for the teacher, the aide, and the child's parent all to be involved in the observations. Often the teacher and aide divide the group in half, each taking primary responsibility for completing the assessment for his or her half of the group. There should be frequent discussions between them to ensure consistency in evaluation.

Chapters Three through Seven of this manual present a more detailed explanation of the task activities the child must perform for the assessment. Each item on the scale is accompanied by a statement of the *Developmental Significance* of that item. The developmental significance for each item is critical. For example, the importance of Item 43 is not simply that the child compares length by "selecting the longer of two sticks." What is important is that in comparing length, specific developmental processes are taking place within the child that are important to healthy development. Similarly, the developmental significance statement for Item 43 says:

> Making comparisons and seeking similarities and differences are important elements in effective problem solving. The ability to differentiate a long object from a short object is one element in this process.

From these developmental significance statements, the person doing the assessment has a basis for understanding the developmental process. Planning will then be done in response to the developmental processes, rather than simply programming activities for the child. The person doing the assessment should have a sense of how to observe children and what the observations mean. This handbook presents information to help the observer structure and interpret the observation.

Almost anyone working with children can readily learn to use the *Humanics National Child Assessment Form*. With the support material in this handbook, the information from the assessment can be used to understand the child's developmental progress and to plan individualized activities to stimulate the child's growth and learning.

WHAT SKILLS DOES THE WORKER NEED TO CONDUCT THE ASSESSMENT OBSERVATIONS?

A few basic considerations will improve the usefulness of the information derived for the results of the assessment. Those who have worked with young children for some time know that there is a skill in observing them. The skilled observer can see the process of development in the child's behavior and is alert to small but significant events. For example, a child in active group play may pause momentarily to assist a child who has been pushed down. Such a brief gesture indicates the child's sense of social awareness and the development of empathy and social concern. The skilled observer is aware of the developmental significance of small bits of behavior because he or she understands the developmental processes the behavior represents. He or she does not merely respond to the behavior.

Prior to conducting developmental assessments, staff and parents should receive training in observation skills. This training should focus on recognizing significant developmental behaviors, understanding the child's present developmental level, and being aware of the developmental processes that are occuring which result in the observed behavior. Chapter One on child development and the developmental sigificance statements presented for each item will be useful in this training.

Before conducting assessments, observers must also be aware of special developmental problems that might appear during the assessment. In monitoring the developmental progress of the child, the alert observer sometimes detects behaviors that signal a special handicapping condition. Chapter Eight includes a description of how to use the developmental assessment as a program-wide screening for handicapping conditions. A list of signals of potential problems with which all observers must be familiar is presented along with suggestions for referral for diagnostic evaluation. Training should also include recognition of the behavioral significance of potential handicapping conditions presented in Chapter Eight.

Programs sometimes focus their first parent meeting on assessment. Parents are given the opportunity to see the *Humanics National Child Assessment Form* and to discuss the items with the program staff. The *H.N.C.A.F.* is relatively simple to administer, and a two-hour parent session provides enough orientation for parents to make meaningful observations when they visit the center to observe their children.

As additional staff training, those using the *H.N.C.A.F.* should be given an overview of the instrument. This overview should also include a discussion of procedures for conducting the assessments, including scheduling, responsibilities, deadlines, parent involvement, and other mechanics of the assessment procedure. This training will be part of the pre-service training since initial assessment is conducted early in the program year. Such training should be integrated with the observation skills training described above, but should focus on specific behavior items on the checklist. It should be emphasized that the specific behaviors on the checklist are significant *only* as indicators of developmental progress. The specific checklist item itself means very little when taken out of context.

It is imperative that teachers understand the developmental process, and they must understand also that the checklist items are only indicators of this process from which teachers may develop meaningful individualized programs. Otherwise, the individualized program becomes merely a series of activities which fail to focus precisely on the basic developmental needs of the child.

WHAT MATERIALS ARE REQUIRED TO CONDUCT THE ASSESSMENT?

Prior to the assessments, supervisors must anticipate the number of children to be assessed and assure that enough copies of the assessment form are available. Since the *Humanics National Child Assessment Form* is based on normal child activities, it does not require specialized equipment or materials to administer. The objects used in the assessment are those normally found in the home or center. Figure IV is a list of materials required for administering the *H.N.C.A.F.* The center director or education supervisor is usually responsible for these pre-assessment arrangements.

FIGURE IV

Materials Required To Administer the *Humanics National Child Assessment Form*

For each child assessed:

1. A second copy of the *H.N.C.A.F.* if parents are to complete one at home.
2. One copy of this handbook for each teacher administering the assessment.

The following materials will be needed for specific *H.N.C.A.F.* items:

ITEM	MATERIALS
20	short book or record
32	picture storybook
34	alphabet blocks or cards
37	small color chart
38	figures of a circle, square, triangle and rectangle; crayon or pencil and paper
39,45	number cards
42,50	crayon or pencil and paper
43	two sticks of obviously unequal length (e.g., 4" and 7")
44	four different sized balls
46	four different colored beads and string
	four different colored blocks
48	beads or small blocks
51	pencil, pen, crayon, fork, knife, spoon
56	balance board 6" wide raised 3" off the ground
57	12" stool

59	12" ball
60	3" ball
62	two 3-piece puzzles
63	figure of a circle; crayon or pencil and paper
65	record player or tape player with recording of rhythmic music
67	two 5-piece puzzles
68	child-sized scissors and paper
71	3" to 4" ball
76	fork and spoon
81	commercially manufactured dress-up dolls such as *Dapper Dan* or *Dressie Bessie*.
88	copy of puppet from Item #42

CONDUCTING THE ASSESSMENT OBSERVATIONS

Information for assessing the child's developmental progress is based on systematic observation of behaviors identified on the assessment form. Gathering the information to complete the *H.N.C.A.F.* will require both informal and structured observation of the child. Actual assessments should take place in the school setting, however, in order to maintain the consistency of the testing environment.

Informal observation consists of noticing relevant aspects of the child's ongoing behavior. Often parents and teachers find that many of the behaviors on the checklist can be observed informally during the child's routine daily activity. For example, some times for informal observation are free play, snack time, small group time, or time on the playground.

Some of the items on the scale require observation of specific behavior that may not occur routinely. In these instances, a special "game time" should be set aside when the child is presented with the individual tasks identified on the instrument. The structured observation should provide complete information for any item not seen during the informal observation.

There is no set rule delineating which behavior should be observed informally and which to structure more formally. Generally, information gathered through informal observation is a more realistic description of behavior and may give a clearer statement of behaviors that "occur consistently" in the child's development. As a guide, activities should be structured for those behaviors that are not observed informally or, in individual cases, for behaviors where there are specific questions or concerns about the child's progress in a particular developmental area. The more the child's schedule allows for a variety of activities during the day, the more opportunity will be presented for informal observation.

Teachers, aides, and parents should get together to share their opinions about each child's developmental level. These discussions lead naturally into individualized planning for the child.

In summary, the *Humanics National Child Assessment Form* is readily useable by those associating with young children. Common behaviors serve as indicators of developmental progress. Training that helps staff and parents build skill in observing child behavior, recognizing tasks identified on the assessment form and relating task mastery to developmental progress, however, will improve the overall usefulness of the tool and the assessment process. It is recommended that the person responsible for staff development provide the above type of training to the staff prior to beginning a program-wide assessment project.

PLANNING FOR THE PROGRAM-WIDE ASSESSMENT

The program director, education supervisor, lead teacher, or other person with administrative responsibility will have to plan and prepare for the assessments. This responsibility is particularly important if the program has a large group of children entering at one time, such as in the fall, where each child needs to be assessed quickly. Figure V is a Supervisor's Planning Guide for setting up the assessment program.

FIGURE V
EDUCATION SUPERVISOR'S GUIDE TO PLANNING THE PROGRAM-WIDE DEVELOPMENTAL ASSESSMENT

1. Determine the approximate number of children to be assessed and obtain enough copies of the instrument for all new children. (The number of children who are being continued for the second year and who began an assessment record the prior year will be subtracted from the number of new copies required.)
2. Get copies of the *Humanics National Preschool Assessment Handbook* for each teacher or aide, or at least one for each center where the assessment will be administered.
3. Design an assessment training session for staff as described in the text of this handbook. (See page 26).
4. Schedule and announce the time for assessment observations and deadlines for completing the assessments. Make assignments to those responsible for each child's assessment.
5. Inform parents of the assessment and invite their participation (see sample letters in Figures I-III). Conduct a parent meeting on assessment if possible.
6. Ensure that all teachers have the necessary materials to do the assessment (Figure IV) and help them develop lesson plans that include assessment-related activities.
7. Conduct assessments and complete profiles for each child.
8. Schedule time for meetings to develop an Individualized Education Program for each child.
9. Monitor and follow up to assure that staff understands what to do and that all do it as scheduled.

USING THE ASSESSMENT RESULTS

After the *Humanics National Child Assessment Form* has been completed on the child, an Individualized Educational Program (IEP) can be developed. Chapter Eight details how to use results of this assessment and presents a sample IEP format based on information in the *H.N.C.A.F.* The developmental significance statements for each item and the related sections on child development in Chapter One of this handbook will help staff write an IEP based on the developmental processes of the child, and not just on the specific behaviors the child has mastered.

The assessment results and the IEP are particularly important for supervisors or others responsible for others who work with the children. The IEP gives a basis for monitoring the staff's progress and effectiveness in designing classroom activities and in working with individual children.

Similarly, the assessment and IEP process can be used to help parents understand at what level the child is functioning and how the activities are related to the child's developmental progress. Through involvement in the assessment and IEP process, parents will see more clearly that the children do not simply come to the center and play, but that the activities in which the children participate have a clear and significant purpose.

Generally, assessments are conducted as early in the program year as possible. It is desirable to wait two or three weeks after beginning the program in order for children to become accustomed to the new environment. Assessments of all children should be completed no later than two months after they enter the program.

The schedule for assessments should be set prior to the beginning of the program year. Most programs set aside a specific time period for assessment. When you are using the *Humanics National Child Assessment Form*, we recommend designating a two-week period during which teachers, aides, and staff can observe the children in daily activities and structure the specific tasks called for in the checklist.

In planning for the assessment, the supervisor should help all teachers structure their lesson plans during the two-week assessment period to include as many of the *H.N.C.A.F.* task activities as possible. The more the teacher plans for these activities in the daily lessons, the simpler it will be to observe the behaviors identified on the form.

FOLLOW-UP ASSESSMENTS

A second formal assessment may be conducted late in the program year for each child, following the same procedure as was followed in the initial assessment, including the parental involvement. The discussion should focus on areas of the child's growth, the developmental level at which the child is now, styles of learning that work best for the child, and a proposed plan for the future. This material should be summarized and made available to those responsible for planning for the child's next Individualized Educational Program.

UNIT II

THE HUMANICS NATIONAL CHILD ASSESSMENT FORM

Chapter 3

Humanics National Child Assessment Form: Social-Emotional Development

ITEMS 1-18

identifies body parts

Points on request to face, arm, leg, or foot.

DEVELOPMENTAL SIGNIFICANCE:

Children listen to the speech of others and learn to copy or pattern what they hear in their own oral language. A critical element in this process is the establishment of meaning for a variety of nouns and verbs. There are strong relationships between the growth of vocabulary and the ability to think and reason.

This activity relates to a most basic aspect of the labeling process in which children are asked to name body parts which are central to an understanding of themselves.

TASK DESCRIPTION:

Children can point to a face, head, arm, leg or foot when asked to do so.

SAMPLE OBJECTIVE:

To establish meaning for a set of words which describe parts of the body.

SUGGESTED ACTIVITIES:

1. Have a *Rag Doll Day* when the children can bring their favorite dolls to school. Have enough dolls available at the center for children who do not own dolls so that each child has a doll to use in Activities 1 and 2. Ask them to point to various parts of their dolls and then to point to similar parts of themselves. Question the children about the similarities and differences between themselves and their dolls.

Today we'll be ragdolls.....

2. Ask the children to sit on the floor and pretend to be like their favorite dolls. They can then pantomime how they would like their dolls to be able to move and compare these movements with the ways in which the dolls can really move. Practice additional vocabulary which describes the movements, actions, or functions of each body part.

3. Use a simple geometric puzzle (such as the one included on the next page) which the group can assemble to show that they understand how the primary parts of the body fit together.

4. For close attention to detail with faces, let children use commercially produced "face paints" to place dots or lines on cheeks, chins, or ears as instructed. These paints are easy to wipe off.

shows feeling

Smiles and shows other appropriate emotional responses.

DEVELOPMENTAL SIGNIFICANCE:

In earlier stages of development, children may demonstrate spontaneous responses which reflect their feelings at any given time. These responses may not be socially appropriate to particular settings. As the process of socialization advances, children learn to express their feelings in ways that match their situation.

TASK DESCRIPTION:

When the child is observed in an instructional or play setting, she expresses a range of emotional responses which are in harmony with the situation. These include anger and tears, as well as joy and laughter.

SAMPLE OBJECTIVE:

To provide for both the release and control of a range of emotions.

SUGGESTED ACTIVITIES:

1. Make a picture file which shows people expressing a variety of feelings. Talk about them and ask the children if they have had similar feelings.
2. Use the examples of "paper plate faces" shown below and have the children color the one that matches their mood. Talk about their reasons for selecting one or the other.

Afraid   Unhappy   Angry   Happy

 **separates from parents**

Separates from parents without reluctance.

DEVELOPMENTAL SIGNIFICANCE:

Many children experience a good deal of insecurity or even fear when placed in new environments. Classrooms are no exception. The setting will be new, fellow classmates strangers, and the teacher an unknown adult. It takes a good deal of self-assurance, confidence, and independence for a child to separate from a parent under these circumstances. For the child to understand that the separation is only temporary, and to begin to relate to the newness of school, shows movement towards independence.

TASK DESCRIPTION:

The child is able to play with others, become actively involved in classroom activities, and respond in a positive way to the teacher without showing undue stress.

I don't want you to leave me ...

SAMPLE OBJECTIVE:

To build an association between home and school, and relationships with others in school.

SUGGESTED ACTIVITIES:

1. Advise parents, in advance, to describe school in a positive and supportive way.
2. Try to find opportunities for teachers to visit children in their homes before school begins.
3. Permit parents to stay in the classroom for a little while during the first day or two. Ask the parents to encourage their children to play with the materials. Tell the parents to increase their physical distance from their youngsters and finally leave.
4. To involve the children in an initial group activity, read any version of *The Gingerbread Man*. Then ask the children to color the outline of a gingerbread man (see next page). They may also try to cut it out.
5. Create a picture file of parents at home and at work. Discuss them with the children.

Gingerbread man

 **relates to adults**

Calls by name two adults on staff. Relates positively to adults, but is not overly dependent.

DEVELOPMENTAL SIGNIFICANCE:

The ability to name teachers and other school workers suggests that the child is able to establish an initial relationship with them. Prior to entering school, most children are able to name a range of people with whom they are familiar. It is a new challenge to name those who are new and unfamiliar.

TASK DESCRIPTION:

In the presence of the teacher, the child is able to call two members of the staff by name.

SAMPLE OBJECTIVE:

To establish relationships with others.

SUGGESTED ACTVITIES:

1. Make name tags for all of the children. Let them tell their names. See how many names of other children they can remember. If desired, use the pattern from the next page. Keep name tags in Kangaroo's pocket.
2. Take photographs of the teachers and staff, and make a bulletin board displaying them. Talk about what each one does.
3. Make name tags for several teachers and staff members. Take the class on a partial tour of the school to "find" the teachers and co-workers and give them their tags.

Kangaroo pattern directions on the next page.

Kangaroo Name Tag Holder

1. Cut 1 piece of brown wrapping paper the size of your door.
2. Draw kangaroo, cut out and laminate.
3. Tie red ribbon around neck.
4. Cut another piece of brown wrapping paper one half the size of your first piece. This is your pocket.
5. Draw legs on the pocket and staple to your kangaroo.
6. Cover staples with brown rick rack if you wish.

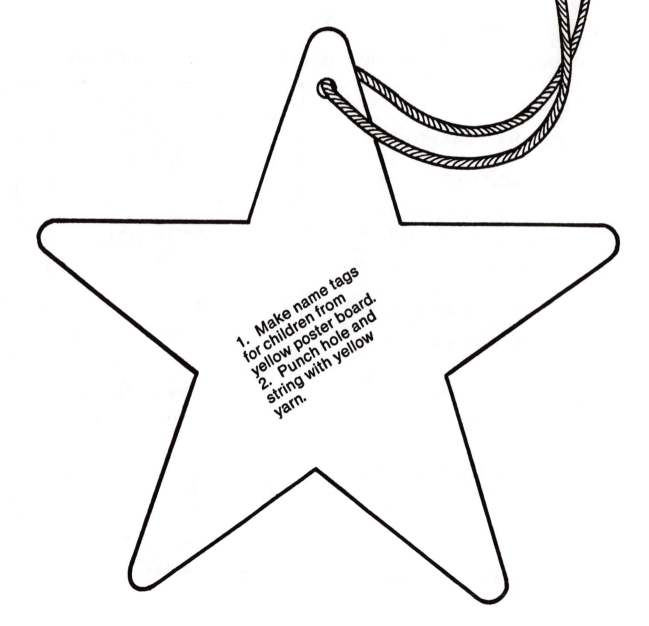

1. Make name tags for children from yellow poster board.
2. Punch hole and string with yellow yarn.

 interacts with children

Talks comfortably with other children.

DEVELOPMENTAL SIGNIFICANCE:

As children develop the need to communicate with others to satisfy personal needs, they also have to acquire the necessary language skills to do so. Beginning conversations may be highly self-centered, but should develop to indicate awareness of the needs, desires, and points of view of others.

TASK DESCRIPTION:

When observing a group of children, the teacher listens to the conversation for evidence of "give and take", politeness, and the ability of each child to participate in the dialogue.

SAMPLE OBJECTIVE:

To develop language competence in conversational settings.

SUGGESTED ACTVITIES:

1. Sing the song, "Here We Are Together."

2. Do the *Pass and Repeat Game*. Find an interesting object. Use an interesting sentence to describe it. Have the first child repeat the sentence and pass the object on to the second child. The second child repeats the same sentence and passes the object on to the third child.
3. Assign children to be monitors and helpers. Make sure that their tasks require communication with others.

6 seeks new experiences

Eager for and seeks out new activities and experiences; exhibits curiosity.

DEVELOPMENTAL SIGNIFICANCE:

Children need to explore an array of activities and experiences which enable them to find new comprehension and understanding of their world. These experiences may also provide a basis for increased self-confidence and independence, and can contribute to positive self-concept.

Mom, this is Rover...

TASK DESCRIPTION:

The child responds enthusiastically to novel experiences and activities.

SAMPLE OBJECTIVE:

To provide learning experiences which foster creativity, curiosity, and self-concept.

SUGGESTED ACTIVITIES:

Have several *Monster Days* during which both realistic and imaginary monsters are dealt with.

1. Read: *Where The Wild Things Are* by Maurice Sendak.
2. Make a clay monster and talk about what it does when it is naughty or nice.
3. Discuss pictures of dinosaurs and ask questions about whether they were monsters or not.
4. Make a volcano. Make up a group story of what might have happened to the dinosaurs if a volcano erupted nearby. What might have happened to their monsters if the *pretend* volcano was *real*?

MATERIALS NEEDED TO MAKE CLAY VOLCANO:

Hand-sized clump of clay for each child.

Water

Paint brushes.

Individual pieces of plastic coated wallpaper.

Black glaze for firing in kiln,

or black paint.

HOW TO:

1. Place clay on wallpaper in front of child.
2. Show each child how to work a few drops of water into the clay clump.
3. Form a cone. Using thumbs, press cavity into cone.
4. Let "volcano" dry thoroughly.
5. Glaze and fire or paint and allow time to dry.

LAVA:

1. Have children mix red food coloring into vinegar.
2. Pour one teaspoon of baking soda into volcano cavity.
3. Add colored vinegar and watch your own eruption.

MATERIALS NEEDED TO MAKE PAPER VOLCANO:

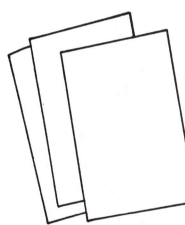

White construction paper

Scissors

Brad

Pattern

HOW TO:

1. Trace volcano on large construction paper.
2. Trace cone on small piece of construction paper.
3. Color outside of volcano black.
4. Color inside red and orange.
5. Color top or head.
6. Cut out top or head.
7. Using brad, attach top to volcano.
8. Each child is now able to make her own eruption.

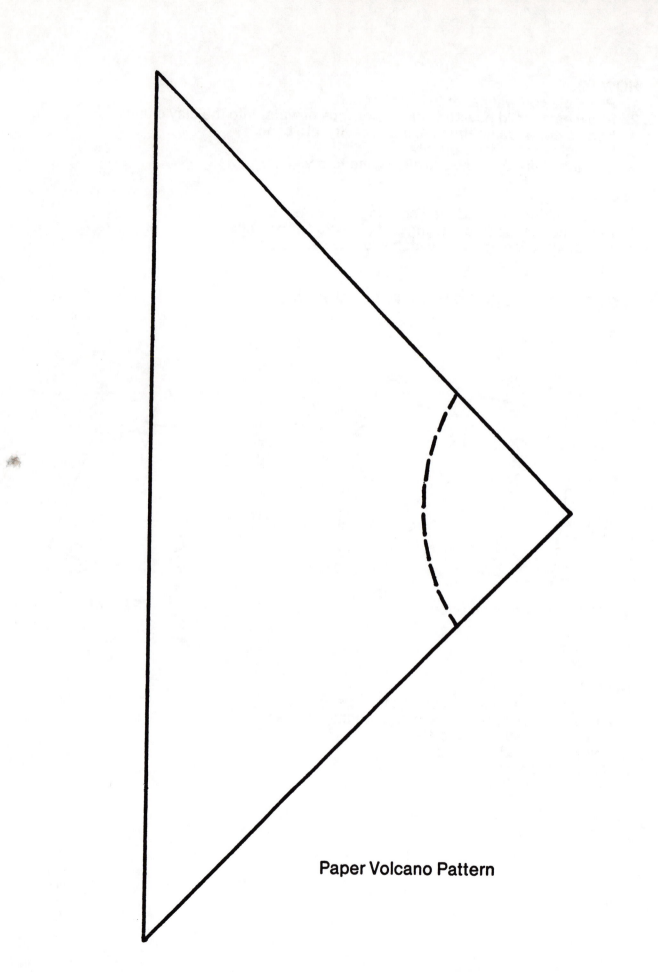

Paper Volcano Pattern

7 maintains interest

Maintains interest in play activity without encouragement from an adult.

DEVELOPMENTAL SIGNIFICANCE:

Very young children need a good deal of variety, encouragement, and attention as they engage in play activities. As interests develop and their worlds become more comprehensible, the amount of time "on task" may be expected to increase. Given interesting and stimulating settings and activities, children may be expected to demonstrate more social maturity by their ability to sustain interest in specific activities.

TASK DESCRIPTION:

When involved in play at a housekeeping corner, art area, or other learning centers, the child will focus on the activities provided without requiring constant attention or reminders to do so.

SAMPLE OBJECTIVE:

To encourage concentration on tasks and activities for increasing periods of time.

SUGGESTED ACTIVITIES:

1. Set up several interest areas or learning centers where children can work alone, or with others, on a variety of tasks. These should include quiet places and active areas.

   ### QUIET AREAS
   A painting corner
   A picture book center
   A "look and think" science area

   ### ACTIVE AREAS
   A block building area
   A housekeeping setting
   A dress up center
   A cut and paste area

2. Provide some activities which can be completed rapidly and others that take an extended time to complete.

 **plays cooperatively**

Plays cooperatively in groups of three or four children.

DEVELOPMENTAL SIGNIFICANCE:

Children move from self-centered or egocentric play to parallel play and ultimately to interactive play. Cooperating, sharing, and developing rapport with others are characteristic of this level of development.

TASK DESCRIPTION:

When observed in a group play activity, the contribution of the child is a definite part of the action. The contribution is not parallel to the action, but an aspect of it.

SAMPLE OBJECTIVE:

To encourage cooperation and interaction.

SUGGESTED ACTIVITIES:

1. Set up a store, post office, or kitchen area in which the children can take on roles and enjoy imitative play.
2. Paint murals based on "story lines" of books read to the class. Arrange for two or more children to work together.
3. Play *Follow the Leader* games.
4. Set up a sand or water area in which two or more children can experiment with filling and emptying containers of differing sizes.

9 modulates voice

Controls volume of speech when
directed and when participating in singing and language games.

DEVELOPMENTAL SIGNIFICANCE:

Young children frequently use inappropriate voice levels in social settings and instructional activities. They are more inclined to be too noisy than too quiet. The ability to match the manner in which something is said to the context or setting indicates increasing sensitivity to the effects of language and self-control in using words.

TASK DESCRIPTION:

When participating in singing activities or language based lessons, the child uses appropriate voice modulation.

SAMPLE OBJECTIVE:

To modulate the voice in acceptable ways during language-related activities.

SUGGESTED ACTIVITIES:

1. Have the children practice quiet and loud sounds:

	QUIET SOUNDS	LOUD SOUNDS
a. Animals:	Mice squeaking Kittens meowing Chicks cheeping	Lions roaring Dogs barking Wolves howling
b. Inside & outside sounds	Water dripping Gentle winds	Waterfall crashing Roaring gales
c. Job sounds:	Brushes sweeping Raking leaves Polishing furniture	Engines clattering Blaring trumpets Drilling holes

2. Play loud and soft notes or music on the piano. The child claps quietly after quiet music and more loudly as the volume of the notes is increased.
3. Talk about the ways in which voices change as emotions change. Use quiet unhappy voices, loud angry voices, and worried, happy, frightened, and excited voices.
4. Read the story of *The Three Little Pigs* and let the children repeat the parts of the wolf and pigs using contrasting voices. As a follow up, let them color the picture of the big bad wolf from the next page.

The Big Bad Wolf

44

**10** persists in task

Stays actively involved in a chosen task until completed or for at least fifteen minutes.

DEVELOPMENTAL SIGNIFICANCE:

Successful completion of this item is a more advanced indication of the persistant "on-task" behavior noted in item #7. It is important to praise these extended efforts. There is a relationship between the ability to concentrate on tasks and complete them successfully, and subsequent success in academic environments.

TASK DESCRIPTION:

When involved in a task such as completing an art project or a mathematics activity, the child focuses on the activity until it is completed, or for an extended period of time.

SAMPLE OBJECTIVE:

To develop concentration on specific tasks for an extended period of time.

SUGGESTED ACTIVITIES:

1. Following story time, praise the children who pay attention.
2. Use puzzles and other games requiring increasing levels of complexity to provide a progression from limited concentration to extended concentration.
3. Give "good citizen" awards or similar badges as rewards for extended attention to tasks. (See next page). Let the children cut them out and color them.

The Good Citizens Award

you are my Sunshine you are my Sunshine....

Your
is Buzzing

cut 2

cut 1

11 shows pride

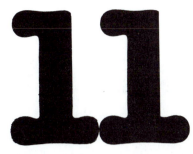

Shows pride in accomplishments or products created. Exhibits confidence in own ability to accomplish simple tasks.

DEVELOPMENTAL SIGNIFICANCE:

Showing pride in accomplishments is an indicator of positive personal feelings and reinforces good self-concept. It is important that positive feelings are reinforced by parents and teachers.

TASK DESCRIPTION:

When the child completes an assignment or creates a product, she will recognize the value of it without depending on the approval of other children or teachers.

SAMPLE OBJECTIVE:

To foster positive self-concept.

SUGGESTED ACTIVITIES:

1. Provide children with simple assignments such as "blow paintings." Praise the completion of the task and make positive comments about some aspect of each painting.
2. After crayoning or drawing activities, ask the children about specific items that they have drawn. Compliment them as necessary.
3. Ask children about their proudest moments or accomplishments.
4. Use the cheer:
   "Zip Zip Zappy
   I am Hip Hip Happy"
   to motivate groups after the successful completion of an extended activity.
5. Experiment with "string art." Dip a string in paint and, holding one end of the string stationary, move the string back and forth between two pieces of paper. Let the children talk about their finished products.

 **shows social awareness**

Shows awareness of and respect for desires of other children.

DEVELOPMENTAL SIGNIFICANCE:

It is critical for children to learn to be aware of others and to cooperate with them. Showing this awareness indicates that the desires, needs, and interests of others are increasing in importance to the individual. They are moving away from almost total concern with themselves into a variety of social interactions in which they need to show respect for fellow students.

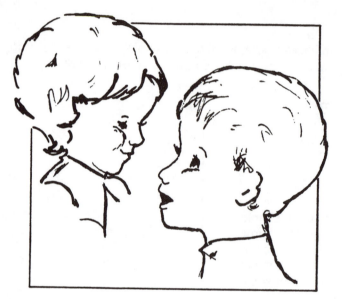

TASK DESCRIPTION:

When another child expresses a specific need or desire, the child responds to that request.

SAMPLE OBJECTIVE:

To develop social awareness.

SUGGESTED ACTIVITIES:

1. Place children in situations where they must share equipment or supplies to complete their tasks. Art and craft activities in which scissors, markers, glue, or paper need to be shared are examples.
2. Passing out napkins, crackers, fruit, or drinks during snack time helps individuals respond to the needs of others.
3. Give out *sweet puffies* for caring behavior. On rarer occasions *sour gruffies* may be called for. (See next page).

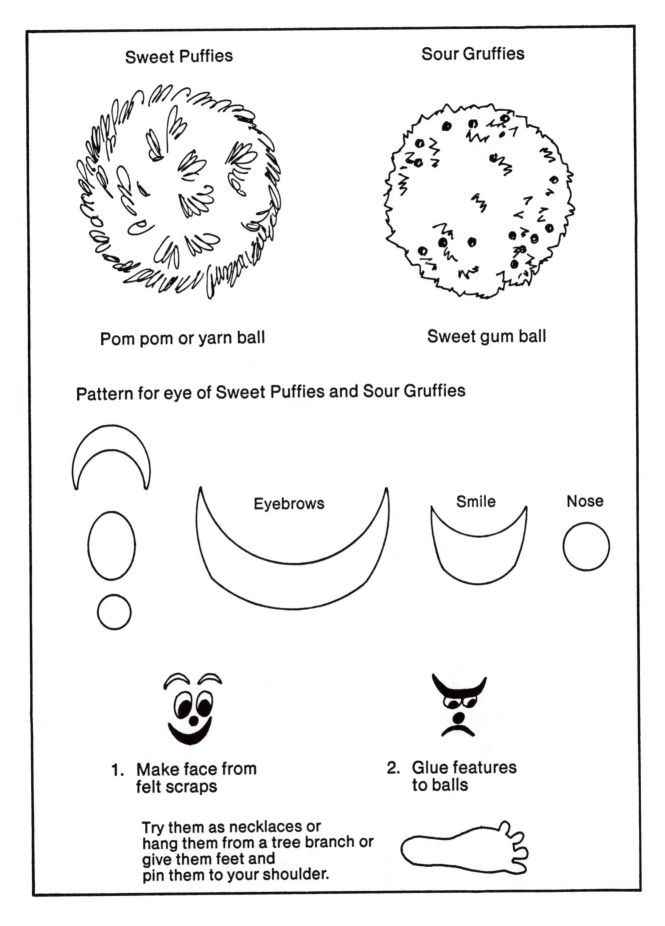

Sweet Puffies

Pom pom or yarn ball

Sour Gruffies

Sweet gum ball

Pattern for eye of Sweet Puffies and Sour Gruffies

Eyebrows

Smile

Nose

1. Make face from felt scraps

2. Glue features to balls

Try them as necklaces or hang them from a tree branch or give them feet and pin them to your shoulder.

protects self

Stands up for own rights and does not permit other children to constantly take unfair advantage.

DEVELOPMENTAL SIGNIFICANCE:

Children must be able to tell others when they feel that their personal rights have been infringed. The ability to do so reflects developing self-concept and social awareness. A child who is unable to stand up for her own rights may be indicating a lack of self-concept and could be taken advantage of by other children.

TASK DESCRIPTION:

When other children seek to take unfair advantage of a child, she is able to stand up for her own rights.

SAMPLE OBJECTIVE:

To enhance self-concept and social awareness.

SUGGESTED ACTIVITIES:

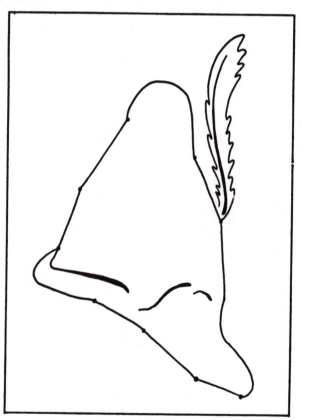

1. Encourage children to express their feelings verbally when problems occur. Talk about: torn drawings, broken toys, unnecessary roughness or bullying.
2. Children enjoy knowing that they have ownership or control over areas or things. Have them stand, drawing an imaginary line around themselves and another around their neighbor. Help them understand that because we like and respect our friends, we do not invade their space or circle. In turn, they will respect our space or circle.
3. Listen to: AR49 *Activities For Individualization In Movement And Music* by Rosemary Hallum and Henry "Buzz" Glass with Edith Newheard, Consultant Educational Activities, Inc., Freeport, New York.
4. *The 500 Hats of Bartholomew Cubbins* by Dr. Seuss tells of a boy who stands up for himself under the most difficult circumstances. Read it to the children, following up with the hat exercise on the next page.

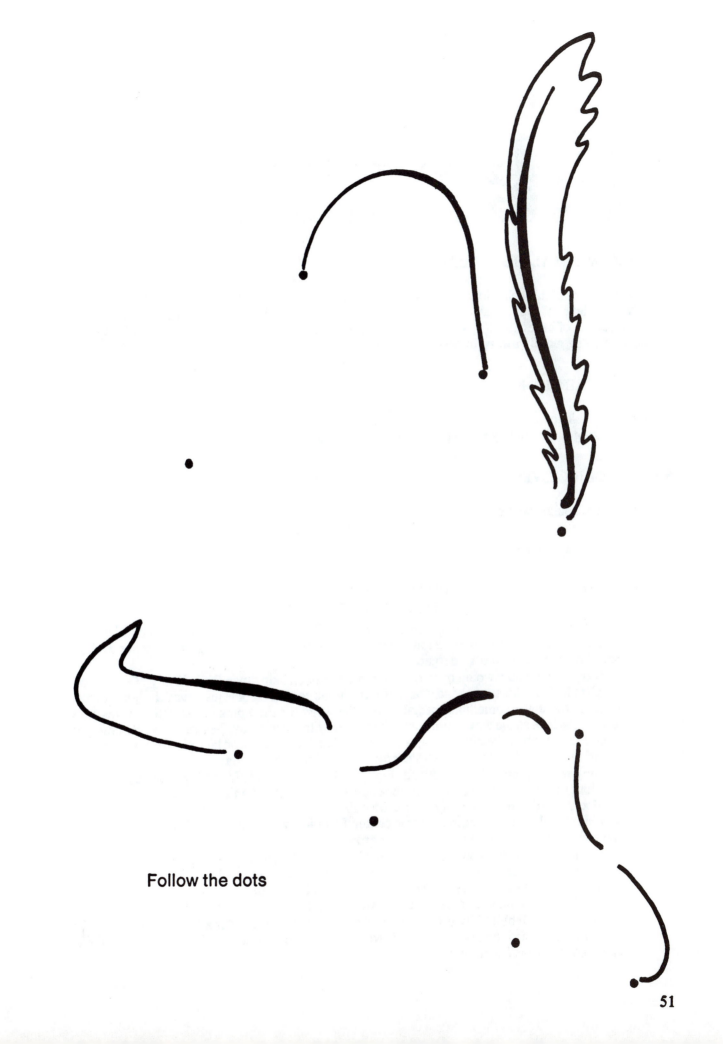

Follow the dots

 **concerned about fairness**

Has concern for fairness in what happens to other children.

DEVELOPMENTAL SIGNIFICANCE:

The existence of this behavior suggests that a child is becoming socially mature. This item is an advanced level of that behavior addressed in item #12 where the child notes the needs and perspectives of others. *Active* sharing and taking turns shows an advance in social maturity beyond being merely *aware* of needs.

TASK DESCRIPTION:

A child is able to actively demonstrate concern for fairness in what happens to others by sharing or taking turns, and by making appropriate oral comments.

SAMPLE OBJECTIVE:

To develop social awareness.

SUGGESTED ACTIVITIES:

1. Read the story of *The Little Pink Apron*:

THE LITTLE PINK APRON

Once upon a time there was a little girl named Debbie. Debbie had lovely blond hair and sparkling blue eyes. Debbie was four. Mrs. Jenkins was Debbie's kindergarten teacher. Debbie *loved* Mrs. Jenkins and kindergarten.

Every day, Debbie would open the door to her school, skip down the hall, say "Good Morning" to Mrs. Jenkins, and head straight for the home center. Debbie just *loved* the home center because there was something special there. She *loved* the little pink apron with red rick-rack and cotton lace all the way around, and she played with it every day. Before she went home, she would always place the little pink apron with red rick-rack and cotton lace all the way around on top of the pretend clothes box so she could find it first the next day.

Jenny was Debbie's favorite friend. Jenny had curly brown hair and big green eyes. Jenny was four too. Jenny always came to kindergarten a little later than Debbie. Jenny would open the door, skip down the hall, say "Good Morning" to Mrs. Jenkins and find her friend Debbie. Debbie was always playing in the home center. Debbie always had on the little pink apron with red rick-rack and cotton lace all the way around.

One morning Debbie could not wake up. Her mother had let her watch *Peter Pan* on television the night before. Debbie did not get to bed until very late. Debbie's mother called and called and called her, but Debbie could not get out of bed for the longest time. She did not feel good. She did not like her breakfast. She was going to be late for school!

Now, Jenny, Debbie's favorite friend, had a good night's rest and made it to school right on time. Jenny opened the door, skipped down the hall, said "Good Morning" to Mrs. Jenkins, and started for the home center.

Oh no!!! Guess what? Debbie was not in the home center. Jenny was sad until she realized that now *she* could wear the little pink apron with red rick-rack and cotton lace all the way around.

Debbie was late for school. She was unhappy and tired. Then she thought of something special. She could not wait to put on the little pink apron with red rick-rack and cotton lace all the way around. It would make her feel better!

Debbie opened the door, ran down the hall, forgot to say "Good Morning" to Mrs. Jenkins and started towards the home center. There was Jenny wearing the little pink apron with red rick-rack and cotton lace all the way around . . .

What do you think happened?

Talk about alternative endings to the story.

    2. Talk about what to do if:

        a. Two children need to use the scissors, but there is only one pair left.

        b. Two children need to use the same ball or doll.

        c. There are not enough morning snacks for all the children.

        d. One child grabs a toy from another child who is playing with it

    3. When problems arise in the classroom, describe them to the children and ask for their help in finding solutions.

APRON I

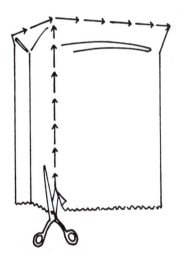

Cut out bottom of paper bag & press out with hand

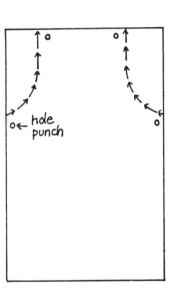

Trace pattern and cut

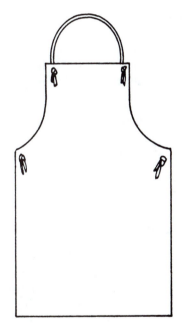

Use yarn or string as ties

APRON II

Cut long strip of crepe paper

Cut out one side of paper sack

Staple to strip of crepe paper

Decorate as you choose

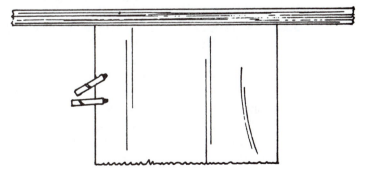

demonstrates responsibility

Takes responsibility for own behavior in
staying within the rules of games and activities.

DEVELOPMENTAL SIGNIFICANCE:

The egocentric activities of young children do not require rule systems other than those imposed internally by a particular child at play. Cooperative play and games with rules require that individuals conform to a scheme or system wich is imposed externally. These group activities demand that the child play within a specified framework or boundary. They involve a sophisticated form of cooperation, advanced social awareness, and control over personal feelings.

TASK DESCRIPTION:

While involved in a game or activity, the child is able to put aside personal needs or desires for the sake of continuing the experience. The teacher, parent, or other children do not need to remind the child of her responsibilities or the proper behaviors necessary to remain consistent with the needs of the group.

SAMPLE OBJECTIVE:

To develop social awareness
To encourage cooperative behavior
To control feelings

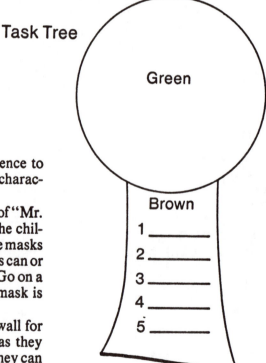

Task Tree

Green

Brown

1 _____
2 _____
3 _____
4 _____
5 _____

SUGGESTED ACTIVITIES:

1. Read *Robber Racoon* by Thomas Lawrence to the children, acquainting them with the characteristics of racoons.
2. On the next page, you will find a pattern of "Mr. Robber". Copy it, making a pattern for the children to trace and cut out. Tape one of these masks to your trash can. Tell the children that this can or litter basket is a "litter nest" for Robber. Go on a litter hunt to fill the can.(Mr. Robber's mask is found in Item 41. See page 106).
3. Pin a "task tree" on a bulletin board or wall for each child Explain to the children that as they complete the "tasks" on the "tasks tree" they can "X" in a space on the task tree. Give the boys and girls 5 tasks to complete per week. Examples of tasks are: puzzles, mazes, games, listening center, and problems to solve.
4. Play *Duck, Duck, Goose.*
5. Talk about the rules in your classroom or home.Why are rules necessary? What would happen if there were no rules?

16 aware of consequences

**Behaves with an awareness
of likely consequences of the behavior.**

DEVELOPMENTAL SIGNIFICANCE:

This item has both social-emotional and cognitive dimensions. It requires that children think about the consequences of their behavior. It builds upon earlier learnings identified in the following items: #12, #13, #14, and #15.

TASK DESCRIPTION:

The child demonstrates through oral communications or actions that she realizes the consequences and responsibilities of her behavior.

SAMPLE OBJECTIVE:

To further develop social awareness, cooperation, and the release or control of feelings.

SUGGESTED ACTIVITIES:

1. Read the *Broken Vase* by Pauline Palmer Meeks to the class. Discuss the spectrum of emotions found here. Ask the children if they can remember if they have had such experiences.
2. Send the children to tables already set up with water colors, water, and paper. Show them the washes used by the artist in the *Broken Vase*. Ask them to use washes of color to identify their feelings as the book is read again.
3. Reinforce this lesson with the puzzle activity on the next page. Trace and reproduce the puzzles. Let the class cut the vases out, reassemble them, and glue them together.
4. Ask the children what they learned about their emotions prior to or during the activity.

17

shows creativity

Contributes original ideas and exhibits flexibility in play and creation of products.

DEVELOPMENTAL SIGNIFICANCE:

In order to develop independence and promote creative thinking, children need an opportunity to make choices, use and practice language, examine relationships, and construct or reconstruct their ideas, in ways that are new or novel to them. The ability to control or modify these elements leads to increasing self-confidence.

TASK DESCRIPTION:

When give a selection of art or craft materials, mathematical equipment, a science kit or language activity, the child shows an ability to manipulate them in new and meaningful ways to himself.

SAMPLE OBJECTIVE:

To promote individual expression and independence.

spoon   Tempra   marbles

SUGGESTED ACTIVITIES:

1. Provide a dress up box. Ask the children to experiment with different combinations of clothes and pretend to be different characters.
2. Read *Christina Katerina and The Box*, by Patricia Lee Gauch at rug time. Christina becomes the owner of a refrigerator box. The children will enjoy all of the creative ways she uses it. Bring boxes into the classroom, or onto the playground, for the children to use to copy these ideas or make up their own.
3. On a large piece of paper, have the children draw a box. Then ask them, "What would you do with your box?" Have the children draw their answers below their box picture. Or, as a child describes her box activities, print her answer on the sheet and read it back to her.

18 exhibits appropriate values

**Exhibits consideration for others,
a sense of humor and self-discipline.**

DEVELOPMENTAL SIGNIFICANCE:

As social relationships develop children may be expected to exhibit caring behaviors for others. This indicates maturing self-concept and increasing attention to the needs of persons in their world.

Humor evolves from the understanding of discordant associations between objects, persons, or events. It suggests a positive caring and spontaneous response to an unexpected happening.

TASK DESCRIPTION:

The child shows increasing levels of positive interaction, friendliness, and good humor, in a variety of group settings.

SAMPLE OBJECTIVES:

To develop social awareness, promote expression of positive feelings, and build self-concept.

SUGGESTED ACTIVITIES:

1. Read the excellent book, *The Giving Tree*, by Shel Silverstein, New York, Evanston, & London, Harper & Row, 1964. It teaches an invaluable lesson in consideration. Read it to the children and ask for their reaction.

2. Sing such songs as "*A Little Song of Life*" by Lizette Woodworth Reese.

3. *Johnny Appleseed* has always been a favorite historical character for boys and girls. The stories told of him bring out his sense of humor and fair play. Read a story or show a film strip about Johnny Appleseed. Let the children assume the role of Johnny Appleseed (with a pot on their heads) and say how they solve problems which arise in the classroom

4. Using the pattern on the next page, have the children learn the "Golden Rule" and talk about what it means.

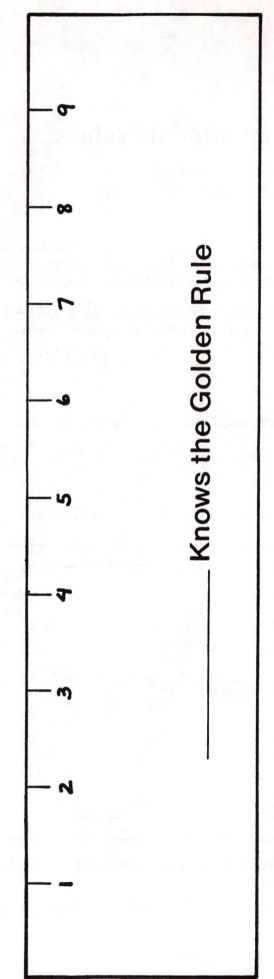

Knows the Golden Rule

The Golden Rule
Treat others the way
you would like them to
treat you!

Paint ruler gold
and glue to cardboard

Chapter 4

Humanics National Child Assessment Form: Language Development

ITEMS 19-36

19 follows directions (I)

Follows a simple direction ("Sit down," "Jump," "Clap hands," etc.)

DEVELOPMENTAL SIGNIFICANCE:

The ability to accurately follow simple directions shows that a child has correctly interpreted oral signals and translated them into meaningful actions. This skill is of primary importance in instructional settings.

TASK DESCRIPTION:

The child sits, jumps, claps hands, walks, or runs when told to do so.

SAMPLE OBJECTIVE:

To develop a specific receptive language skill.

SUGGESTED ACTIVITIES:

1. Play simple games such as *Simon Says*.
2. Use records which contain instructions for children to clap, dance, jump, or turn around.
3. Use the *Arrow Activity*. Point it up, down, or to the side, depending on the direction in which the children must move. It can be used to show level or direction.

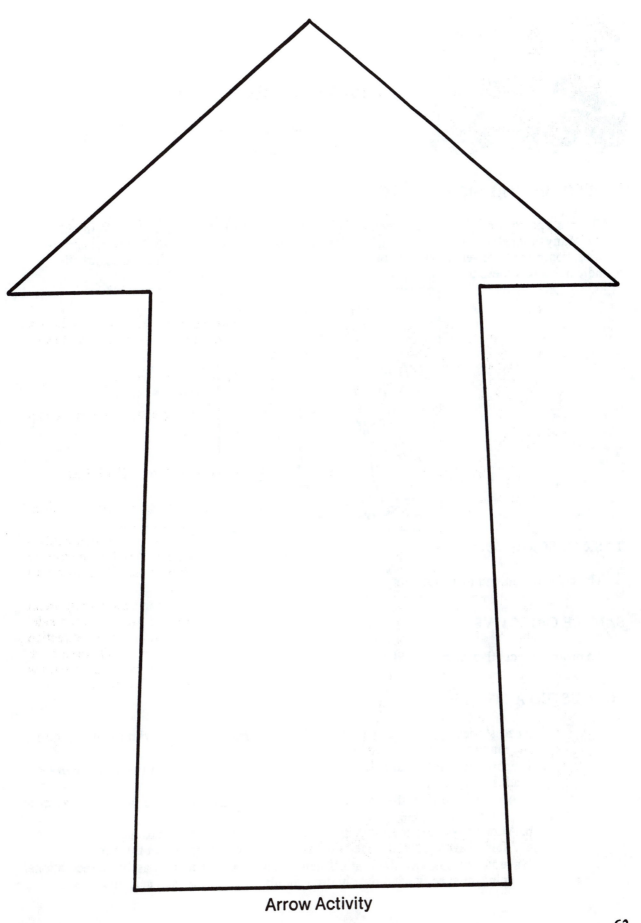

Arrow Activity

extended listening

Attends to a short story which is read directly,
or played on tape or record.

DEVELOPMENTAL SIGNIFICANCE:

There is a positive relationship between good listening ability and subsequent success in reading. Many other elements of classroom learning require careful attention to directions, instructions, comments, conversations, and oral presentations made by teachers. Increased attention
indicates a readiness to learn.

TASK DESCRIPTION:

The child will attend to a short story.

SAMPLE OBJECTIVE:

To promote receptive language skills.

SUGGESTED ACTIVITIES:

1. Read stories with interesting illustrations that may be shared with the group during
   the reading.
2. Prepare the children to think about specific or general parts of the story *before* it is
   read. Example:
   a. After I have read the story, I want you to tell me about the part that was most
      interesting to you.
   b. After I have read the story, I want to see if you can retell it to me.
   c. After I have read it, tell me about the most exciting person in the story.
3. Have story records available at a listening station. Use them for passive or recreational
   listening, or specify what the children should listen for in each selection.

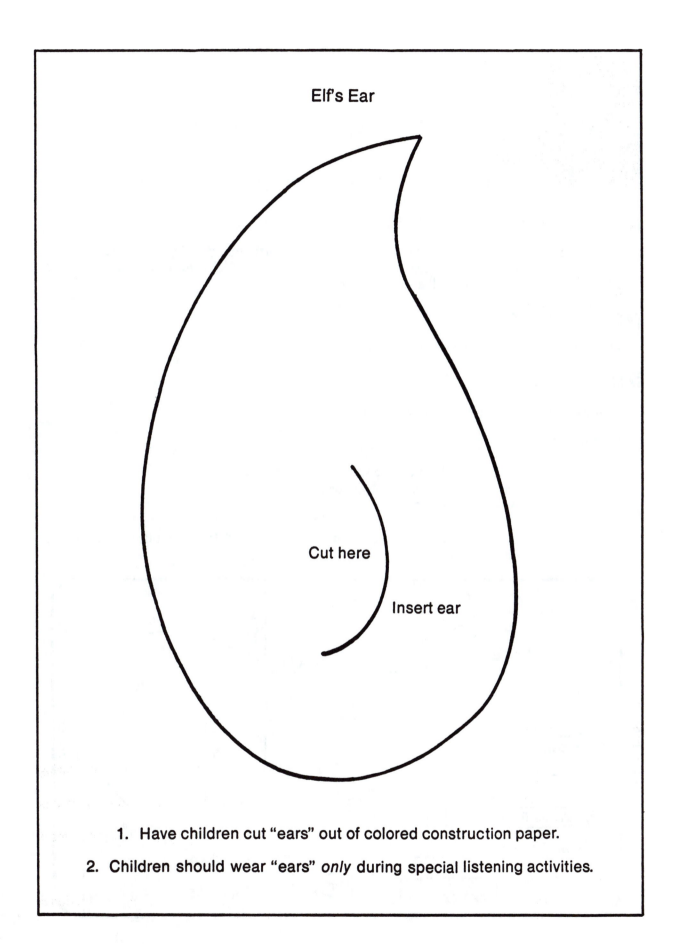

Elf's Ear

Cut here

Insert ear

1. Have children cut "ears" out of colored construction paper.

2. Children should wear "ears" *only* during special listening activities.

follows directions (II)

Follows three or more successive directions in order.

DEVELOPMENTAL SIGNIFICANCE:

This is an advanced version of item #19. The difference lies in the number of specific directions to be followed. The intent is to increase the number of directions, which in turn requires greater attention and the ability to recall a short sequence.

TASK DESCRIPTION:

The child follows a sequence of three directions.

SAMPLE OBJECTIVE:

To develop further receptive language skills.

SUGGESTED ACTIVITIES:

1. Ask the group to follow three successive directions:
   a. Stand up — turn around — sit down
   b. Step — jump — hop
   c. Stand — stretch — squeeze hands (into fists)
2. Set out maze pathways using the arrows from Item #19. Give three directions for following this maze.

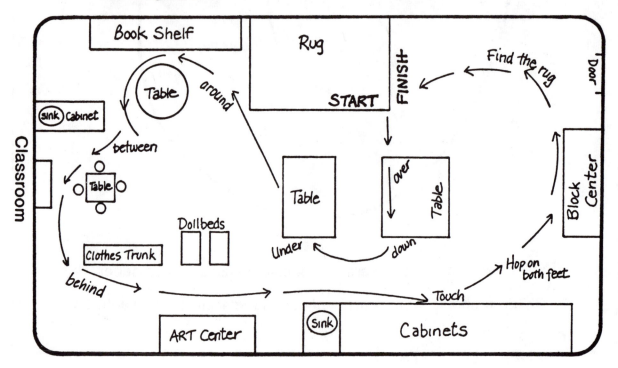

 **discriminates between words**

Identifies similarity or difference
between five pairs of words presented orally.

DEVELOPMENTAL SIGNIFICANCE:

Many words in English sound similar to each other. When children are able to discriminate between pairs of words which have the same beginning sound but different middle or final sounds, they demonstrate increased skill in auditory discrimination.

TASK DESCRIPTION:

When a child is presented with five pairs of words which are similar or different, she is able to say whether the words in each pair are the same or not.

SAMPLE OBJECTIVE:

To develop skills in auditory discrimination.

SUGGESTED ACTIVITIES:

1. In one on one situations, say pairs of words to a child. Ask if the words are the same or different. Examples:

    Cut — Cup   Cap — Cake
    Pin — Pen   Hat — Hot

2. In group settings, play similar and different notes on the piano. Ask the children if the notes are the same or not.

3. Later on, begin rhyming games where the children have to listen to the end of words in order to rhyme them:

    a. Use nursery rhymes: *Georgie Porgie*

      Georgie Porgie pudding and pie,
      Kissed the girls and made them
      When the boys came out to play,
      Georgie Porgie ran ___ ___ ___.

    b. Have the children cut the blackbird and the pie out of construction paper using the patterns on the next page. Make an eye for the bird with a hole puncher. Tie a piece of black yarn through it. Fold the bird and slip it into the pie. Repeat the rhyme together. At the appropriate moment, have the children pull the birds out and let them fly (like small kites) around the room.

    c. *Jack Be Nimble* — Allow the children to cut out the pattern of the candlestick. Give them the opportunity to share the rhyme with a friend. One child should hold the candle while the other jumps over it.

    d. Use sentence completion exercises:
      The man is tall. The boy is ___.

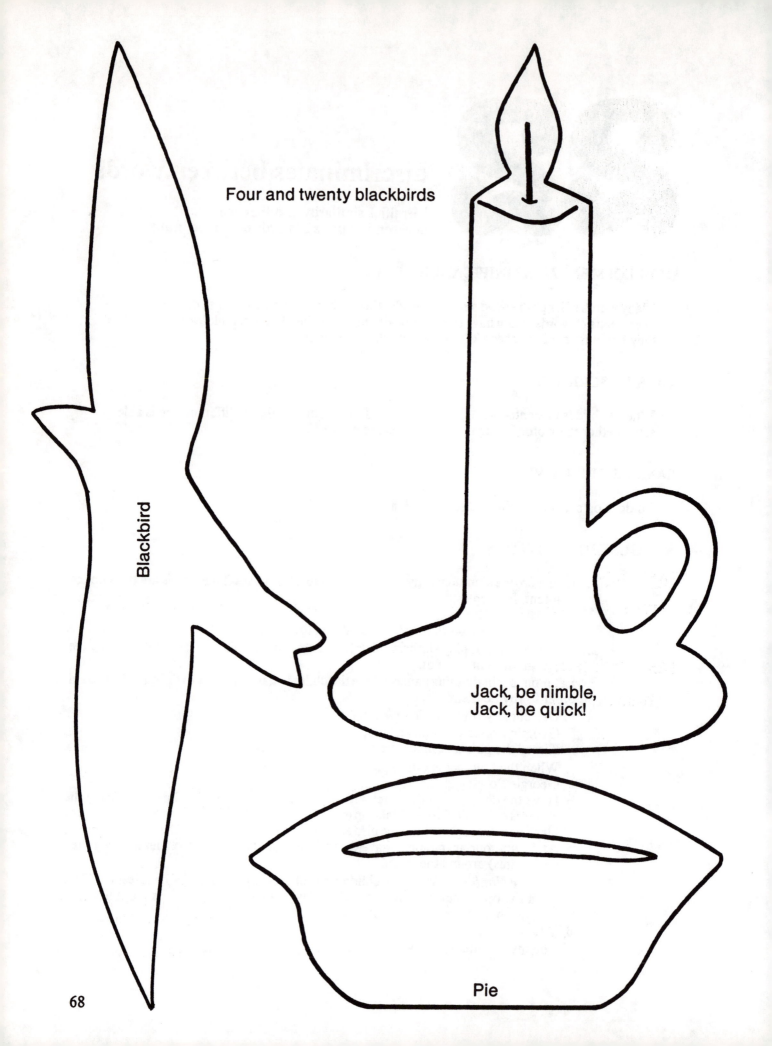

Four and twenty blackbirds

Blackbird

Jack, be nimble,
Jack, be quick!

Pie

68

23 labels objects

Names objects in the environment.

DEVELOPMENTAL SIGNIFICANCE:

The ability to name objects provides information that the child is associating words with the items that they represent. This association is a basic and critical element of language development.

TASK DESCRIPTION:

When she is shown five common objects from home or school, the child names each one correctly.

SAMPLE OBJECTIVE:

To develop oral language skills.

SUGGESTED ACTIVITIES:

1. Make a collection of small common objects from home and school. Pass them around a circle of children for them to look at and feel. Ask about the name of each item. Talk about their other attributes: color, size, texture, weight, and shape.
   Example:

balls	books
blocks	scarves
shoes	hats
spoons	crayons

2. Make a collection of pictures and prints of common objects from magazines. Ask the children to name one or more of the items in each picture. If desired, use the illustration on the next page.
3. Show the group a picture book. Talk about the subject of each illustration.

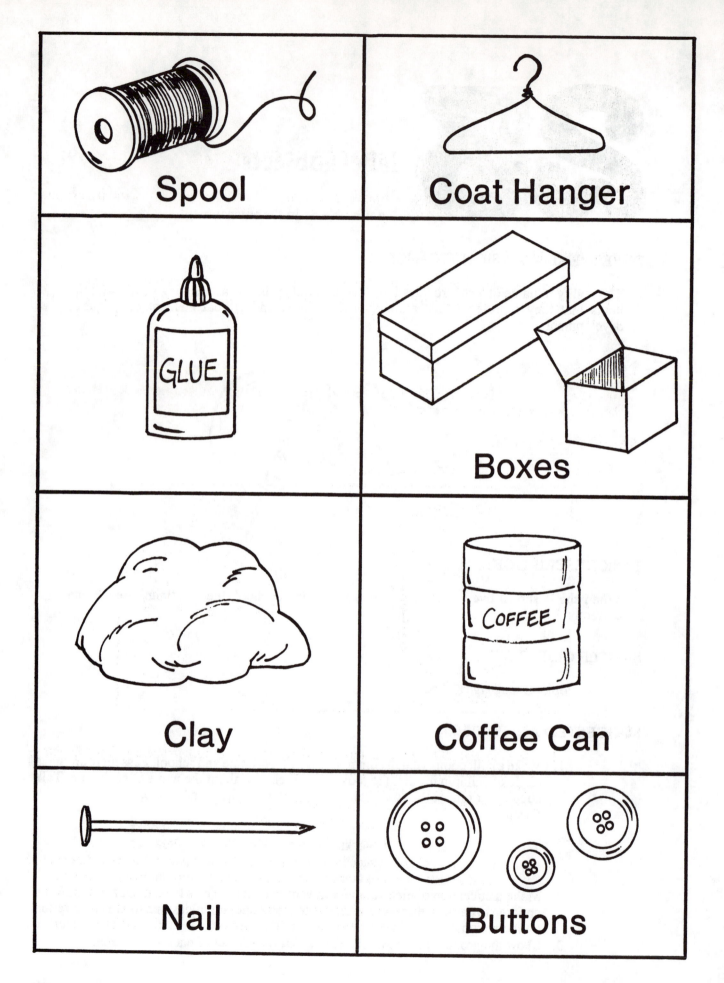

Spool

Coat Hanger

Glue

Boxes

Clay

Coffee Can

Nail

Buttons

24 speaks informally

Speaks effectively in short conversations and in response to questions.

DEVELOPMENTAL SIGNIFICANCE:

As oral language facility increases, the range and variety of possible responses expands. Meaningful and effective speaking may approximate brief sentences, although there are considerable differences between oral and written English. Exact parellels should not be expected.

TASK DESCRIPTION:

In conversations with other children or adults and in responses to questions, the child expresses her thoughts or ideas in a manner that is readily understood by the listener.

SAMPLE OBJECTIVE:

To develop effective expressive language.

SUGGESTED ACTIVITIES:

1. Provide several learning centers or activity areas where speaking is an integral part of the children's work. Investigative science corners, block building, housekeeping, or dress up areas are examples.
2. Model more accurate language as necessary. For example:
   > Child: "Have cookie?"
   > Teacher: "Yes, you may have a cookie."
3. Make the house of *Peter, Peter, Pumpkin-Eater*. (See next page). Each window should suggest a different room in a home (bedroom, kitchen, bathroom, living room). Locate magazine pictures of each, and paste them in the windows. Ask the children to talk about them. Now find pictures of five to ten articles found in each room. Cut these out and laminate them. Have pairs of children discuss where the articles should be placed.

Peter's House

Cut along dark,
solid lines

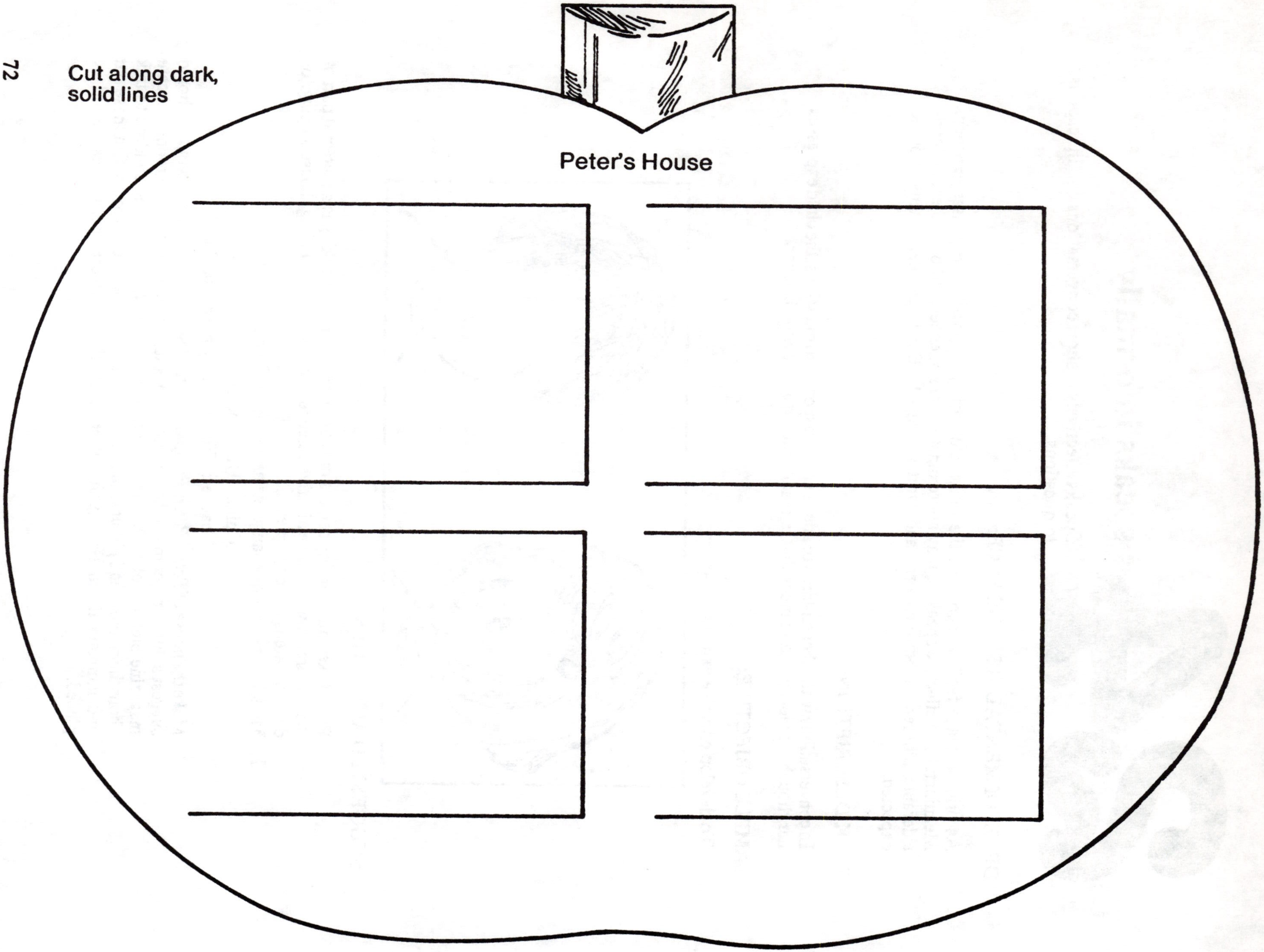

 initiates conversation

Takes leadership role in beginning a conversation.

DEVELOPMENTAL SIGNIFICANCE:

The ability to initiate a conversation indicates that the child has sufficient confidence in her own language facility, and in the person to whom she is speaking, to exchange a few words. For many children this is a spontaneous activity most of the time.

TASK DESCRIPTION:

In everyday situations, the child begins spontaneous conversations with others.

SAMPLE OBJECTIVE:

To support expressive language skills.

SUGGESTED ACTIVITIES:

1. Encourage children to speak softly with one another at meal times or snack times.

2. Circle time provides an excellent opportunity to reinforce this particular skill. Ask one child to leave the room. She should then knock on the door. The class should tell her to "Please come in." The teacher tries *not* to become the dominant force but asks, "Who are you and why are you here?" The class will follow her lead and repeat the question. The child should answer the teacher with her name and add something interesting. The class may then ask Who? What? When? Why? questions. Other children take turns leaving the room and the class repeats the activity.

3. Use the whole classroom to hold a "mini-car race" as a surprise activity. Using the activity on the following page, lay out a race course on the floor of your classroom. Let the children watch your activities, but *make no comment*. Then show the children how to "drive" down the course by pretending to be a race car and making the sound of a racing car as you trot or walk quickly along the race course. Then invite the children to participate in the race. Ask them to describe their imaginary race cars. Note the level of verbal interaction between the players.

START

FINISH

1. Fold around 2 popsicle or craft sticks and glue.

2. Use tacky or play dough as base.

3. Make 3 flags
   a. yellow caution
   b. red starting
   c. checkered

4. Glue to popsicle or craft stick

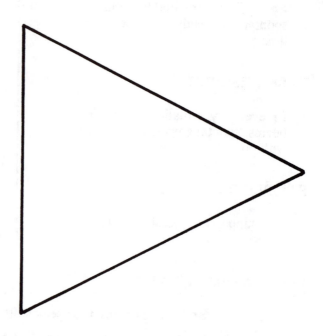

5. Cut off long piece of brown wrapping paper.

6. Draw a line down the middle of the paper.

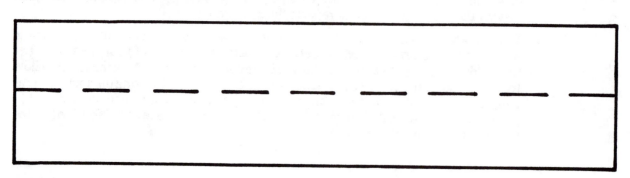

26

speaks more extensively

Holds a conversation, or shares a report,
which lasts for one or two minutes.

DEVELOPMENTAL SIGNIFICANCE:

This is an extension of item #24. The significance lies in the range of vocabulary used, the increasing length of utterances, and the ability to sustain speech for an increased amount of time.

TASK DESCRIPTION:

In conversations with others, and in giving oral reports, the child is able to sustain speech for one or two minutes.

SAMPLE OBJECTIVE:

To facilitate extended oral language.

SUGGESTED ACTIVITIES:

1. Make "show and tell" a frequent feature of classroom life.
2. Place two or more children in problem-solving situations which require conversations. The candle and paper bag experiments which follow are examples.

LET'S EXPERIMENT

A.
1. Light a candle.
2. Cover with jar.
3. What happened?

B.
1. Blow up a paper bag.
2. How do you feel?
3. Pop the paper bag.
4. What happened?

asks questions

Asks questions appropriate to the situation.

DEVELOPMENTAL SIGNIFICANCE:

As the ability to ask questions is an effective way of obtaining information and assistance, it is an important element in the learning process. Questioning ability suggests that the child may be curious, need clarification, or be inquisitive. The child's understanding the relationships between questions and answers also illustrates a more advanced facility with language.

TASK DESCRIPTION:

Observe the child in a variety of situations. Does she ask questions of other children, teachers, or other adults?

SAMPLE OBJECTIVE:

To develop the expressive language skills involved in asking questions.

"Where are you going my little girl, little girl?"

SUGGESTED ACTIVITIES:

1. Model the desired behavior by asking questions of children and encouraging them to do the same.

2. Having given instructions to the class, remember to ask them if they have any questions about their work.

3. Complete the *BAG GAME*. The pattern on the next page shows one half a bag. Make multiple copies and have each child cut out two of them and decorate them. Staple each child's pair together. Another way to make the bag is to use a manila envelope, manila folder or a "by 16" sheet of paper. Each child pretends to be going to visit a special place or special person. The other class members ask questions until they guess where the child is "going." The children may also pretend to be carrying something important, special, or secret in their bags. The members of the class try to guess what the bag contains.

Place on Fold

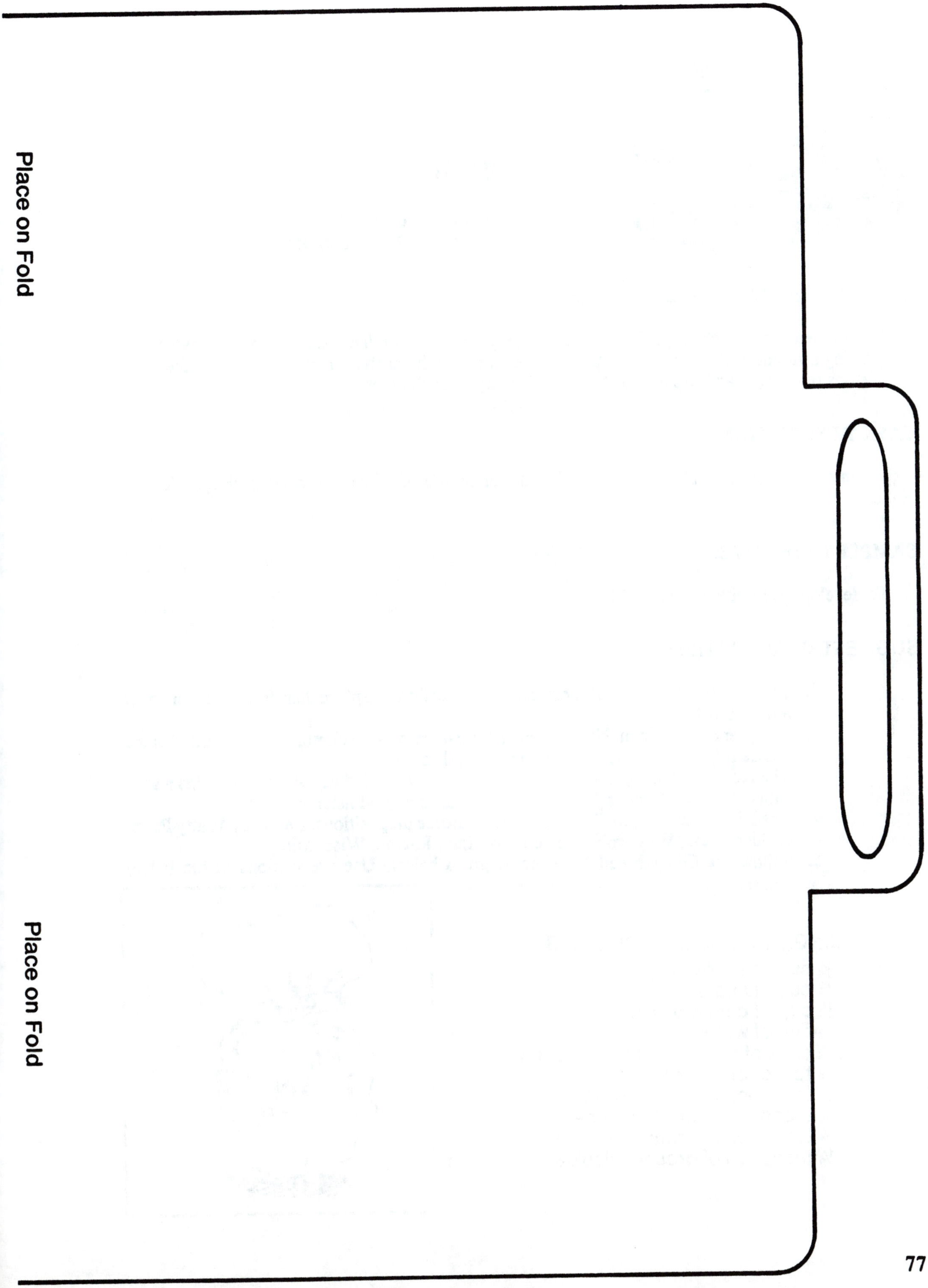

Place on Fold

28 uses prepositions

Uses prepositions in describing relationships of one object to another.

DEVELOPMENTAL SIGNIFICANCE:

Comprehension of such prepositions as *at, by, in, from, with, under, beside,* or *on,* indicates growing awareness of relationships. Children learn to see themselves in relationship to other persons or objects, and to see objects in relationship to each other.

TASK DESCRIPTION:

When asked to place a block on, under, beside, or on top of a box, the child is able to do so.

SAMPLE OBJECTIVE:

To develop expressive language skills.

SUGGESTED ACTIVITIES:

1. Take two objects, such as blocks, and ask the children to place them beside, on, or under a third block.
2. Use prepositions in making up games for use on outside climbing equipment. "Stand beside it," "go under it," "climb on it," and so on.
3. The record by Georgiana Liccione Stewart: *Heel, Toe, Away We Go* contains a song called "Glow Worm on My Shoulder." This is a good listening song.
4. Read *The Little Engine That Could* to reinforce prepositions. Retold by Watty Piper, Golden Press, Western Publishing Co., Inc., Racine, Wisconsin.
5. Follow the Gingerbread Man recipe given below. Use prepositions in the baking process.

GINGERBREAD MAN COOKIES
½ cup of shortening
½ cup of sugar
½ cup of dark molasses
½ cup of water
2½ cups of unsifted all-purpose flour
¾ teaspoon of salt
½ teaspoon of baking soda
¾ teaspoon of ground ginger
¼ teaspoon of ground nutmeg
¼ teaspoon of ground allspice

METHOD:

1. In a large saucepan or electric fry pan, heat shortening, sugar, molasses, and water until the shortening is melted. Remove the pan from the heat and let the mixture cool.
2. In a medium sized bowl, stir together the flour, salt, baking soda, ginger, nutmeg and allspice, mixing them well. Add this mixture to the molasses mixture you made in Step 1 and mix well. Now you have made dough. Wrap it in wax paper.
3. Chill the dough for 2 hours or longer in refrigerator.
4. Have adult turn on the oven to 375° F.
5. Lightly grease a baking sheet.
6. Divide the dough into 3 portions. Put 2 away until you are ready to use them.
7. Sprinkle a light coating of flour on a bread board and rolling pin. Then roll out the dough with the rolling pin until it is about ¼" thick.
8. Put your gingerbread man cookie cutter on the dough and press. Repeat until you have used up all the dough.
9. Use a spatula to transfer the gingerbread man to the greased baking sheet.
10. Bake in the oven for 10-12 minutes. Cool slightly, then remove from baking sheet and place on a wire rack to finish cooling.

Makes 12-14 gingerbread men.

REFERENCES:

KIDS COOKERY
A "Learn to Cook Book for Children"
From McCormick Shilling
Gingerbread Cookie Hands

CUP COOKING
Individual Child-Portion Picture Recipes
By Barbara Johnson
Illustrator: Betty Plemons
Early Educators Press
3120 Maple Drive, NE
Atlanta, Georgia 30305

uses adjectives

Understands and uses adjectives and contrast words (opposites) correctly.

DEVELOPMENTAL SIGNIFICANCE:

There are two elements involved in this item. The ability to use adjectives enhances, elaborates, or clarifies descriptions of objects, moods, settings, and actions. The ability to use "opposites" makes it possible to compare and contrast them. Both elements are part of an elaborate set of language processes through which children are able to express themselves with greater fluency and flexibility. The aim is to help children communicate more precise meanings in speech.

TASK DESCRIPTION:

When asked to describe what something is like, each child is able to use an appropriate adjective as part of an oral response. They are also able to substitute words which create opposite meanings to those used in these responses.

SAMPLE OBJECTIVE:

To express more precise meanings in describing and comparing objects, moods, settings, or actions.

SUGGESTED ACTIVITIES:

1. Concentrate on sensory activities which allow the children to describe how things smell, look, feel, sound or taste.

They are up, down and all around... I'm going to step on one!

a. Place some herbs or spices in jars and let the children smell them and talk about the ones they like or dislike.

b. Present pictures from magazines which show people in contrasting moods and discuss them.

c. Make a "feely box" and fill it with objects which are dissimilar in shape and texture. Ask the children to describe what they can feel.

d. Fill small boxes or similar containers with sets of different objects which make a range of sounds. Talk about the differences between them.

e. Have a "taste in the dark session" in which each child wears a blindfold while trying to describe the taste of three kinds of food.

f. Take the children onto the playground for a great *Bubble Blowing Bash*. Ask them to describe the colors, sizes, shapes, and movement of their bubbles.

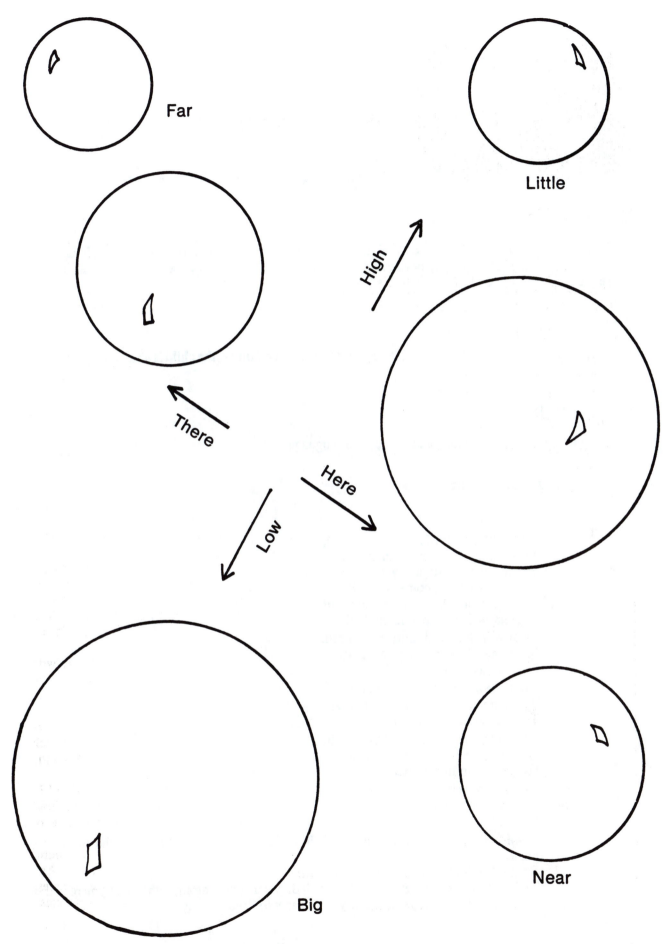

Far

Little

High

There

Here

Low

Near

Big

30 exhibits auditory memory

Repeats song or finger play from memory.

DEVELOPMENTAL SIGNIFICANCE:

Listening and remembering are critical elements of the communications process. In this instance, the child must listen, memorize and repeat. Constant repetition of a song or finger play is required before the child can reach this level.

TASK DESCRIPTION:

After listening to a song or finger play and practicing it several times, the child is able to sing it or demonstrate it from memory.

SAMPLE OBJECTIVE:

To develop auditory memory and expressive language skills.

SUGGESTED ACTIVITIES:

1. *Two Little Bluebirds*

   Two little bluebirds sitting on a hill,
   One named Jack, one named Jill.
   Fly away Jack, fly away Jill,
   Come back Jack, come back Jill.
   Two little bluebirds, sitting on a hill,
   One named Jack, one named Jill.

   Four little bluebirds sitting on a hill,
   Two named Jack, two named Jill
   (Repeat as in first stanza)

   Six little bluebirds sitting on a hill,
   Three named Jack, three named Jill.
   (Repeat as in first stanza.)

   Eight little bluebirds sitting on a hill,
   Four named Jack, four named Jill.
   (Repeat as in first stanza.)

   Ten little bluebirds sitting on a hill,
   Five named Jack, five named Jill.
   (Repeat as in first stanza.)

2. Reinforce success in repetition with Blue Bird Badges, as shown on the following page.
3. Read *This Is the House That Jack Built*.
   Tell the children to listen carefully. Ask if they can follow along with you as you read the story. Within five days, most of your class will "read along".

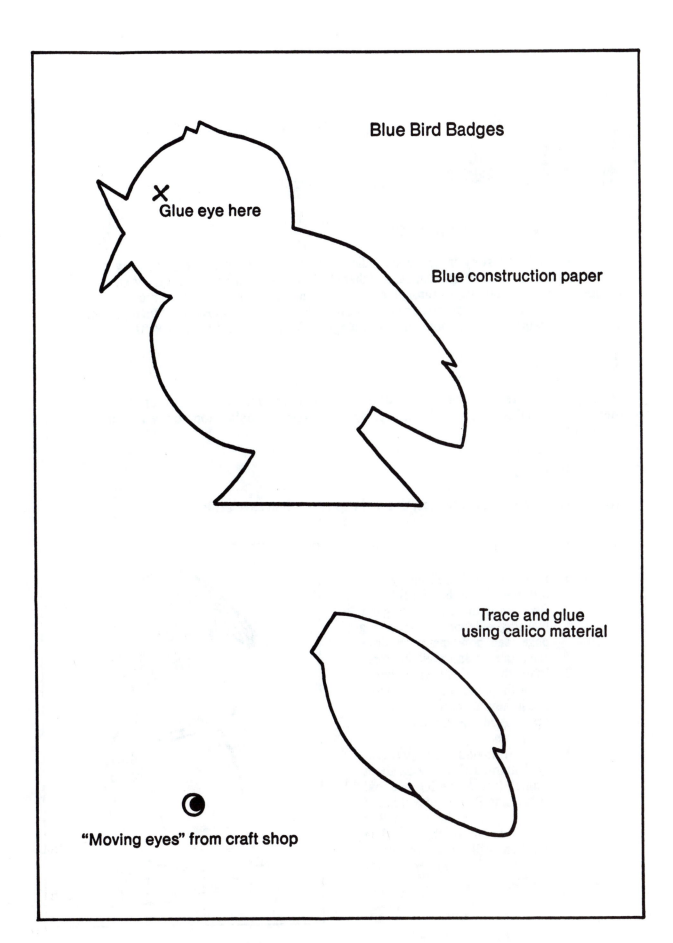

Blue Bird Badges

Glue eye here

Blue construction paper

Trace and glue
using calico material

"Moving eyes" from craft shop

sequencing and retelling

Retells a simple story in sequence.

DEVELOPMENTAL SIGNIFICANCE:

A child's retelling a story in sequence indicates that she has satisfactory memory and an understanding of logical relationships, and that she has gained meaning from the text. Having created a set of mental images through attentive listening, the child is able to reconstruct the story, and retell it to show comprehension. This item does not presuppose constant repetition of the story. It demonstrates a more advanced stage of development than item #30.

TASK DESCRIPTION:

Having been told a simple story over a period of approximately five minutes, the child can retell the story in logical order. The task can be completed in one to one situations, or by individuals in group settings.

SAMPLE OBJECTIVE:

To develop memory and both receptive and expressive language skills.

SUGGESTED ACTIVITIES:

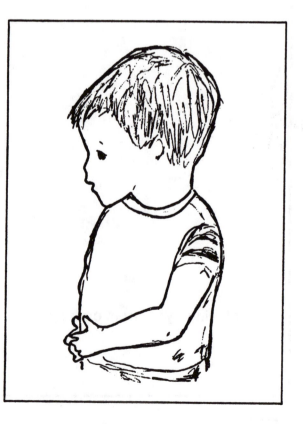

1. Read *They Were Tired Of Living In A House*, by Liesel Moak Sporpen to the class. Using the learning aids on the following page, see how many children can sequence and retell the story.
2. Play the *"Direction Game"* Give the children 3 directions. See if they can carry them out in order. Add one more direction each turn.
3. Read *Strangers Bread*, by Nancy Willard. This is a book about a small boy delivering one loaf of Russian Pumpernickel bread to a lady and the things that happen to him on the way. The children will enjoy trying to retell this tale in sequence without help.

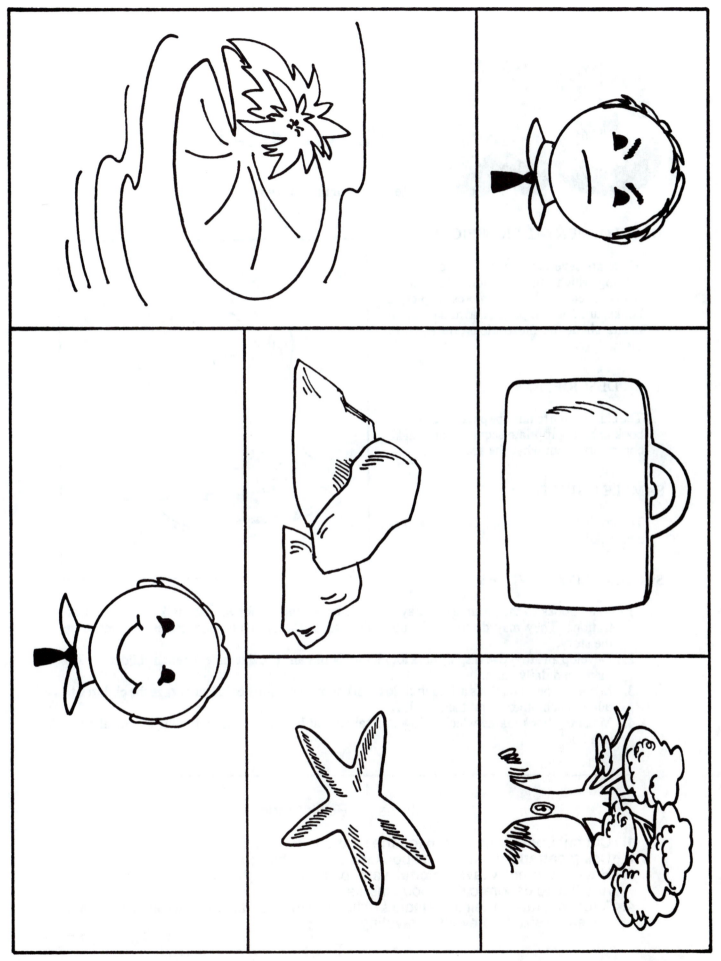

32 exhibits reading interest

"Reads" a picture story book.

DEVELOPMENTAL SIGNIFICANCE:

There are several important aspects of pre-reading which enable children to become ready to read. Taking an interest in picture books, turning their pages, and making comments about the illustrations are some of them.

TASK DESCRIPTION:

The child is able to turn the pages of a picture book in an appropriate sequence and make comments about what she sees.

SAMPLE OBJECTIVE:

To develop receptive and expressive language skills.

SUGGESTED ACTIVITIES:

1. Read books to the group every day. Provide opportunities for them to talk about the illustrations. They may discuss individual pictures or the sequence of pictures that make up the story.
2. Develop an attractive display area for picture books and provide time for each child to look at them on a daily basis.
3. In one-on-one situations ask each child to talk about a picture book. Encourage the children to talk to each other about their books.
4. Make the book marks which follow and talk about how they help in finding a special place in a book.

Directions for Book Mark

1. Cut out book mark pattern (on the next page).
2. Using pattern, cut individual book marks from burlap.
3. Have children weave colorful yarn pieces through the burlap with plastic needles to decorate their book marks.
4. After decorating their book marks, children can glue the burlap to pieces of felt of the same size to prevent unraveling.

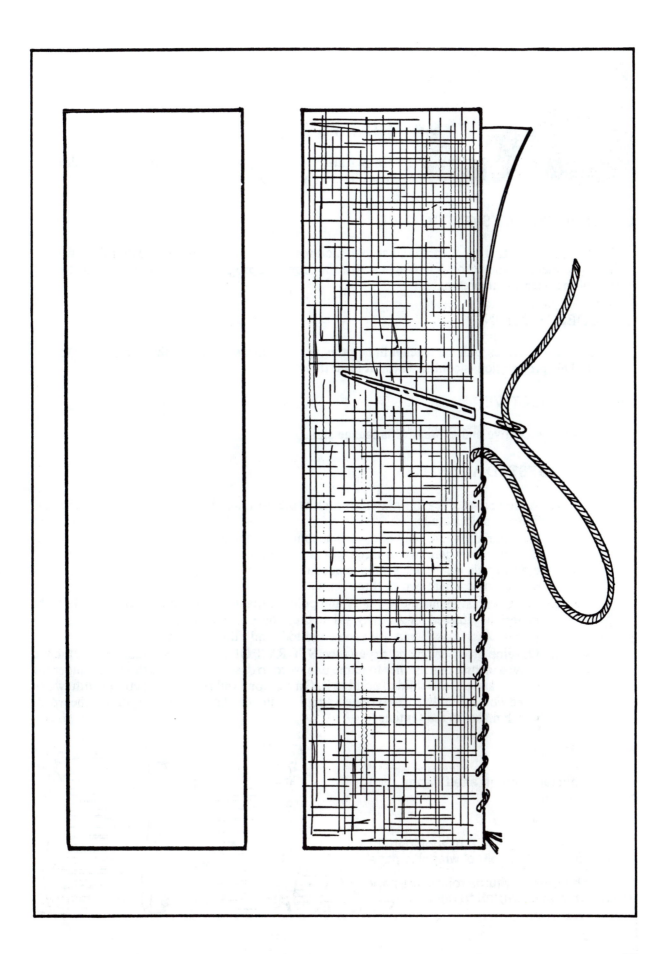

33

knows reading progression

Knows and exhibits appropriate reading progression from left to right and top to bottom.

DEVELOPMENTAL SIGNIFICANCE:

The focus of this item is on words rather than pictures. Children need to become familiar with the movement of words from left to right across the page, and progression of sentences from the top of the page to the bottom.

TASK DESCRIPTION:

The child cooperates with the teacher in pointing at words in a sentence as they "read" left to right. This progression is continued for at least three lines.

SAMPLE OBJECTIVE:

To develop receptive and expressive language skills.

SUGGESTED ACTIVITIES:

1. Acquire a set of reading materials such as picture books which use relatively few words. They should include:
   a. Materials where only one word accompanies the picture.
   b. Materials where two or three words accompany the picture.
   c. Materials where one sentence accompanies the picture.
   d. Materials where two or three lines of print follow the picture.
2. Work with students individually and point to the words while reading them. Use the materials gathered for Activity #1 in the progression shown.
3. Repeat Activity #2 and ask each child to "read" the words along with you.
4. Develop group language experience STORY ROLLS as illustrated. Let each child draw a picture and ask her to name one word to describe it. Write this word under the picture and tell the child to point to it. On a second roll repeat this activity with two or three words. Finally, try to create a simple sentence. Ask the child to point to the words which make up the sentence.

STORY ROLLS

Write a special story on shelf paper, using class participation.

Let the class decorate.

Tape the ends of the sheet of shelf paper to cardboard tubes from rolls of wrapping paper.

Let the children take turns rolling the paper up as you read down, left to right.

34 knows alphabet

Recognizes and names letters of the alphabet on sight.

DEVELOPMENTAL SIGNIFICANCE:

Children need to understand that words are made up of letter shapes that are written down or printed in upper and lower case forms. They are symbols which represent sounds. While this item concentrates on naming the letter shapes, it is a prerequisite to learning the sounds which accompany each letter.

TASK DESCRIPTION:

The child is able to name all of the upper and lower case letters of the alphabet when they are presented to her in random order.

SAMPLE OBJECTIVE:

To promote memorizing and receptive and expressive language skills.

SUGGESTED ACTIVITIES:

1. Teach children alphabet songs.
2. Make up 26 "alphabet books" where all the words in each book begin with an "A", "B", "C", etc. Cut out pictures to accompany each word.
3. Take a tour of the classroom or school hall to look for labels and signs. Take particular notice of the first letter on each sign.
4. Give the children letter shape outlines to color and talk with them about words which begin with each letter as they color it.
5. Talk to the class about the letters in their own names. Write down the names of the persons in each child's immediate family. Ask individuals to identify the letters which make up each name.
6. Let the children construct upper case letters using the recipe which follows. When the letter shapes are done, let the children trace them on paper.

7. See if the children can draw the upper case letters with their fingers in a sand tray.

PLAY DOUGH

2 cups of flour

1 cup of salt

4 teaspoons of cream of tartar

2 tablespoons of oil

2 cups of water

Food coloring

Combine all ingredients together. Mix well.

Cook at medium heat or 300° in electric frying pan, stirring constantly until mixture follows spoon.

Turn out on floured area.

Knead until cool.

Make the letters of the alphabet with coils of play dough.

Bake letters in slow oven for 20-45 minutes, depending on the thickness of the letters, until done.

uses imagination

Can use imagination to create a simple story with some logical sequence.

DEVELOPMENTAL SIGNIFICANCE:

It is difficult to define imagination in a precise fashion. In this instance, it suggests that the child can devise and express a very simple short story. In all probability this story will parallel a story told by a parent or a teacher, or will copy a piece seen on television. It is a matter of taking information that has been learned elsewhere and expressing it in words alone, or words and action.

TASK DESCRIPTION:

In play situation involving dress-up boxes, housekeeping or puppets, the child is overheard relating a simple story. Alternatively, the child is given a stimulus, such as a picture, doll or other object, and asked to make up a story about it. The story may be as short as four sentences which are stated in a sequence that makes sense.

SAMPLE OBJECTIVE:

To develop thinking and expressive language skills.

SUGGESTED ACTIVITIES:

1. As a stimulus have several *Railroad Days*. Sing songs and read stories about trains.
   a. Cut out some kerchiefs for the children.
   b. Make a "maze" of railroad tracks by laying out masking tape on the floor in a railroad track pattern. Let the children walk the "tracks" pretending to be the engineer driving over the rails.
   c. Make two rows of chairs to represent the inside of a railroad car. Give all the passengers a ticket. Let the children take turns at punching the tickets with a hole puncher.
   d. Set up several small groups and ask the children to make up their own railroad stories using their properties from (a).

plays roles

Play activity involves pretending to be another recognizable person (e.g., I am a fireman, I am a nurse, etc.)

DEVELOPMENTAL SIGNIFICANCE:

In this item children need to show an ability to engage in role taking. The characters they explore may be real or fictitious. In completing this activity they show evidence of imitating language, moods, actions and movements of real and imaginary persons.

TASK DESCRIPTION:

To develop informal language and movement.

SUGGESTED ACTIVITIES:

1. Talk about community helpers such a doctors, nurses, policemen and firemen. Ask the children to pretend to be one of these people for a few seconds. Use hats or other properties (such as the Fireman's Hat shown on this page) to support the action. Show children pictures of various hats, such as the illustration which follows, and ask, "Who would wear these hats?"
2. Talk about favorite characters from books read to the class. Ask the children to pretend to be one of these characters for a few seconds.
3. Talk about jobs that the children can do at home and pantomime these activities.

Who would wear these hats?

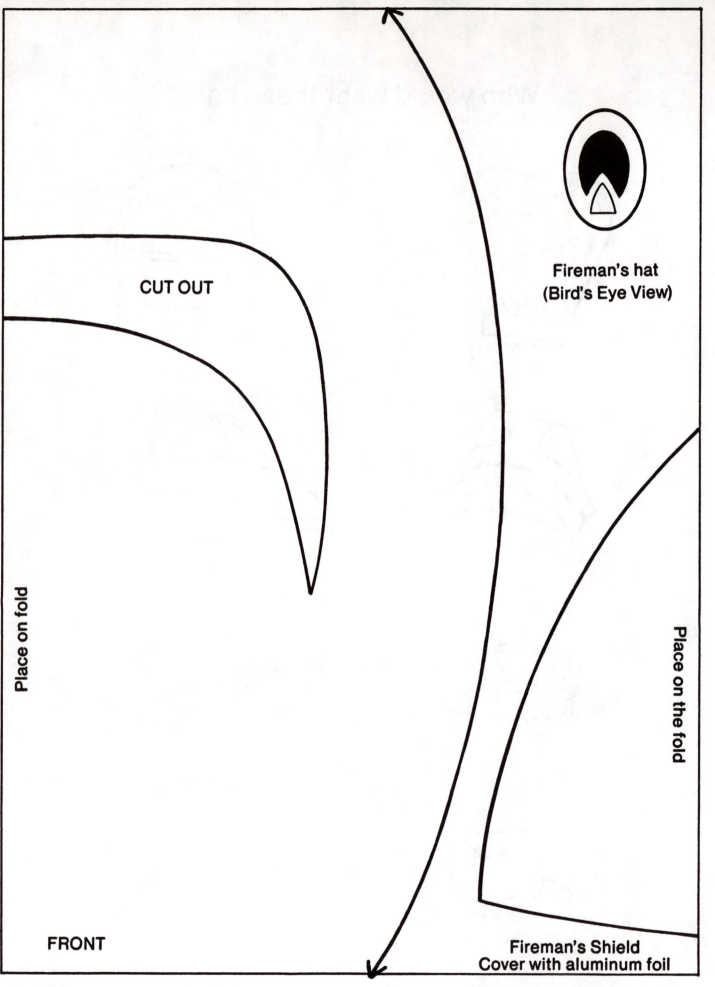

CUT OUT

Fireman's hat
(Bird's Eye View)

Place on fold

Place on the fold

FRONT

Fireman's Shield
Cover with aluminum foil

Chapter 5

Humanics National Child Assessment Form: Cognitive Development

ITEMS 37-54

visual discrimination with colors

Differentiates between four similarly
shaped objects by noting their differences in color.

DEVELOPMENTAL SIGNIFICANCE:

Children rely heavily on their senses to understand their environment. One aspect of visual learning requires discrimination between colors. This skill enables children to note an additional attribute of objects. Knowledge of "color words" provides a way of thinking about single objects more comprehensively, and acts as a method of classifying or grouping sets of similar or dissimilar objects. The accurate use of these adjectives in oral language suggests increasing versatility and fluency.

TASK DESCRIPTION:

When shown four similarly shaped objects in four different colors, the child recognizes and states that their colors are different, and names each color.

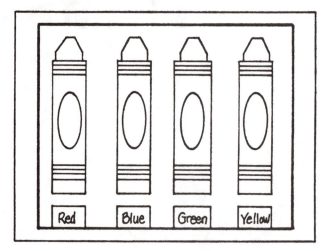

SAMPLE OBJECTIVE:

To develop visual discrimination and thinking skills.

SUGGESTED ACTIVITIES:

1. Listen to the record *Basic Skills Through Music*, Volume II — Parade of Color.
2. Using the activities from the following page, have the class pair matching colors and name them.
3. Play *Color Bingo*, either of the homemade variety or the manufactured form. Playing this game gives the child newfound confidence in discrimination between colors and thinking skills.

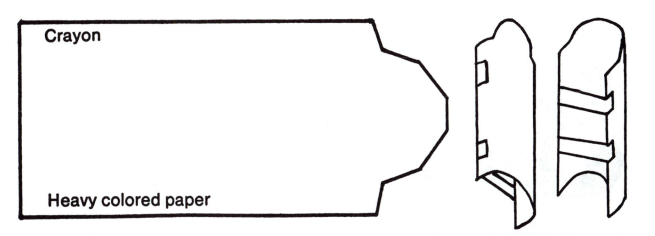

1. Cut basic crayon from heavy colored paper. Curve "crayon" and secure with tape as shown.

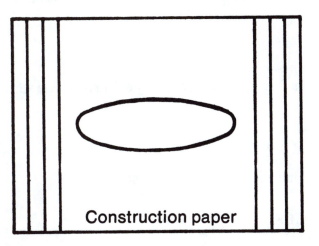

2. Make crayon label from colored construction paper for each basic color and paste to "crayon."
3. Tape "crayon" to a piece of poster board. Tape pockets underneath.
4. Use this poster as a learning aid.

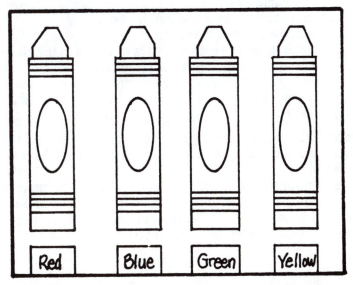

Slip real crayons into the pockets under the matching colors.

identifies shapes

Identifies the following shapes:
circle, square, rectangle, and triangle.

DEVELOPMENTAL SIGNIFICANCE:

The ability to identify basic shapes is another aspect of visual discrimination. The child must note differences in form, build visual memory for each item, and remember the name associated with each shape.

TASK DESCRIPTION:

The child is able to identify a circle, square, triangle, and rectangle when they are shown to him.

SAMPLE OBJECTIVE:

To develop visual discrimination between basic shapes.

SUGGESTED ACTIVITIES:

1. Introduce the children to one shape at a time. Cut the basic shapes out of construction paper, cardboard, wood, plastic materials or fabrics. Make each shape in a variety of sizes.

   For each individual shape (such as the circle):

   a. Show that circles can be made in many sizes.
   b. Make circle name tags.
   c. Trace around circle shapes and cut them out.
   d. Feel around the edges of the circle.
   e. Find other circle shapes such as plates or clocks in the classroom.
   f. Make circle shapes with fingers, hands, or arms.
   g. Play a *Pass and Repeat* game: *Teacher to Child A*: "Sam, this is a large black circle. Its edges are rounded. Pass it on." *Child A to Child B*: "Julie, this is a . . ."

2. After several of the shapes have been introduced:

   a. Make all the shapes with fingers, hands, or arms. Repeat the activity in pairs.
   b. Place a mixture of shapes on a table. Ask a child to take out only the squares, or circles, etc.
   c. Cut and paste shapes on pattern picture (see illustration on next page).
   d. Use shapes made out of thicker materials in a *Feel and Shape* game. Place the shapes in a feely bag and have the children identify them by touch alone.
   e. Arrange similar shapes on a flannel board in order of size.

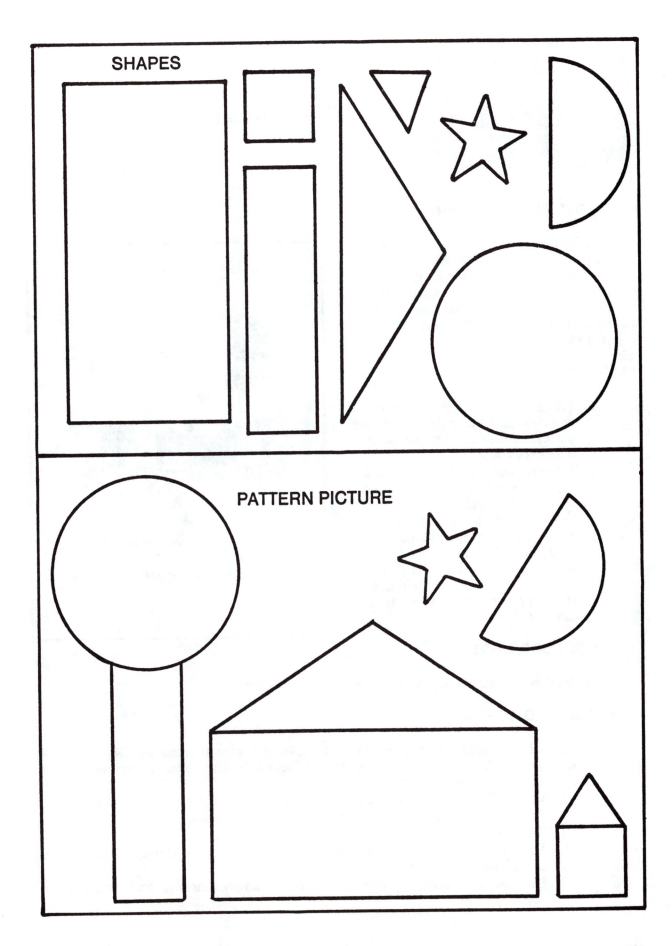

SHAPES

PATTERN PICTURE

classifies objects (I)

Sorts objects into sets,
matching objects according to color, shape, or size.

DEVELOPMENTAL SIGNIFICANCE:

Classification of objects into sets requires that the child recognize common attributes of groups of similar or dissimilar items, and can organize them accordingly. Color, shape, or size are among the common attributes of objects and form bases for the creation of categories.

TASK DESCRIPTION:

1. When shown two similar squares and two similar triangles, the child places them in two sets based on differences in *shape*.
2. When shown four differently shaped objects, two of one color and two of another, the child sorts them into two sets based on similarity of *color*.
3. When shown four objects which may be different in color or shape, but where two are obviously large and two are very small, the child sorts them into two sets based on similarity of *size*.

Look at all those rocks!

SAMPLE OBJECTIVE:

To develop problem-solving skills through sorting activities.

SUGGESTED ACTIVITIES:

1. Give the child a box of mixed buttons and several separate containers. Have the child sort out the buttons on the basis of color. Repeat the activity on the basis of size, and again on the basis of shape.
2. Use packages of mixed nuts and separate them on the basis of shape or size.
3. Play lotto games which require matching objects or colors.
4. Sort wooden blocks into categories based on shapes.
5. Make a collection of socks or mittens. Mix them up and then sort them out on the basis of size, shape, and color.
6. Use classroom dolls, toy cars, or blocks and arrange them in order according to size.

Become Rockhounds

1. Take children on a rock hunt. Have them collect pebbles to small rocks.

2. Turn a half gallon milk carton on its side and cut it lengthwise with matte knife or razor blade. Wash rocks with liquid soap and water in the halved milk carton.

3. Glue dark paper inside a styrofoam meat tray.

4. Have the class classify rocks into sets according to color, shape, or size, and arrange them in the styrofoam trays.

5. Have a "Rock Show" and invite another class.

6. Have the children tell their visitors what they have done.

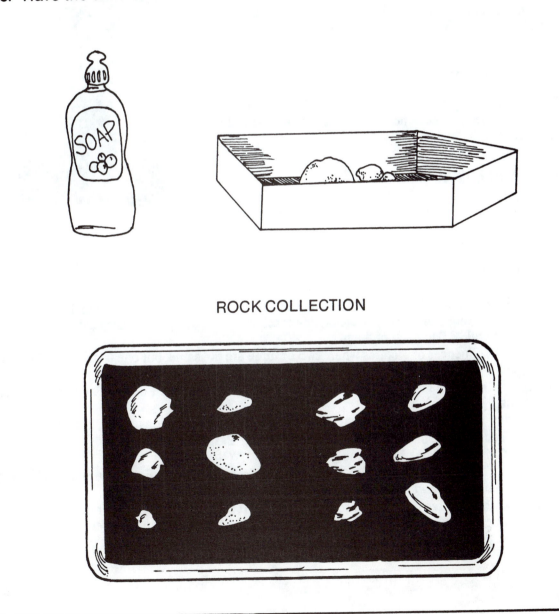

ROCK COLLECTION

 **40** understands number concepts (I)

**Understands the number concept "one";
recognizes and names the numeral "1" on sight.**

DEVELOPMENTAL SIGNIFICANCE:

Demonstrating an understanding of the number "one" indicates that the child comprehends the difference between an individual unit and several units. Naming the numeral "1" shows that the correct label has been associated with it. It is important that the numeral "1" as a symbol for the concept of "oneness" is understood.

TASK DESCRIPTION:

When shown a single object and several different numerals, the child correctly selects the numeral "1" to represent the individual item.

SAMPLE OBJECTIVE:

To build associations between the numeral "1" and the concept of "oneness".

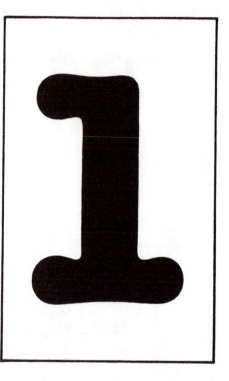

SUGGESTED ACTIVITIES:

1. Have a *"One" Hunt* where the children look around the room to find single examples of objects, e.g., one sink, one clock, one teacher's desk, one pencil sharpener, etc. Tape the numeral "1" to each of them.
2. Use sequences of pictures where two or three are the same, but one is different. Have the child point out the one that stands alone.
3. Explain to the children that they are all different from each other. They are "one of a kind".
4. Play a *Pass and Repeat* game with individual objects (crayons, dolls, blocks, etc.).
   Teacher to Child: "I have one green crayon. Pass it on."
   Child to Child: "I have one green crayon. . ."(Repeat)
5. Talk about "oneness" during snack times and other activities. Everyone needs to have one cup of juice or water, one napkin, one carrot stick, and so on.
6. Let the children cut out and color the acorn. At another center, have children cut out and color the squirrel parts, and put them together with a brad. Use the poem to reinforce the concept of "oneness."

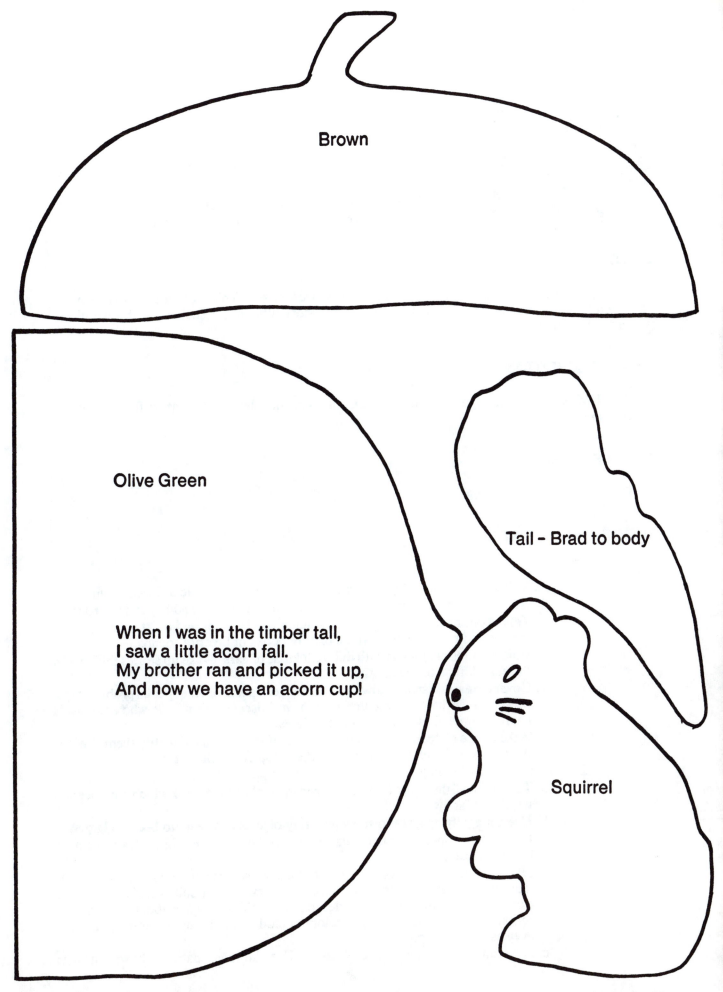

Brown

Olive Green

Tail – Brad to body

When I was in the timber tall,
I saw a little acorn fall.
My brother ran and picked it up,
And now we have an acorn cup!

Squirrel

103

knows the five senses

**Can name the body part(s) associated
with the five senses; e.g., "We see with our eyes."**

DEVELOPMENTAL SIGNIFICANCE:

Children learn the names of body parts at an earlier time (See Item #1). This is a more advanced item which requires children to understand the special sensory functions associated with several parts of the body.

TASK DESCRIPTION:

The child can point to her eyes, ears, nose, mouth and skin, and identify the sensory function of each one.

SAMPLE OBJECTIVE:

To develop sensory awareness.

SUGGESTED ACTIVITIES:

1. Discuss ears and hearing.
    a. Talk about all the things that we can listen to, from music to insect sounds.
    b. Be very still and listen for sounds inside the classroom and beyond the room.
    c. Talk about happy sounds and sad sounds, loud sounds and quiet sounds, gentle sounds and rough sounds. Make picture books of favorite sounds.
    d. Find pictures of animals with different kinds of ears. Make up stories telling why the ears differ from each other.
    e. Cover the ears. Listen to how sounds change. Talk about the special problems that people have when they are unable to hear. Discuss how people who are hard of hearing, or deaf, overcome their problems.
    f. Make a tape of "common" sounds and see if the class can identify them. Record the voices of the children and see if the group can identify them.
2. Discuss eyes and seeing.
    a. Talk about all the things that can be seen in the classroom. Ask which are close and which are far away.
    b. Use a magnifying glass to show how tiny objects can seem to become larger.
    c. Use a telescope, or binoculars, to show how distant things can seem to become closer.
    d. Have a child stand up for everyone to look at. Ask the children to remember as much as they can about the way that child looks. Ask the child who is "it" to hide from the others while they try to describe everything they can about her. This description may include clothing, colors of clothing, patterns on clothing, hairdo, eyeglasses and so on.
    e. Have children go on "Blind Walks." Use the mask pattern shown on page

106.

3. Discuss the nose and smelling.
   a. Obtain some "scratch and sniff" labels and ask the children to identify the smells.
   b. Put an assortment of liquids and solids which have distinctive smells in baby food jars. See if the class can identify them.
   c. Put different cosmetic scents on cotton balls. Ask the children to talk about these fragrances.
   d. Talk about favorite smells and least favorite smells.
   e. Pop popcorn, or something similar, which the children think smells wonderful.
   f. Find pictures of animals with differing noses and make up stories about their differences.

4. Discuss the mouth, tongue, and tasting.
   a. Show the group several small dishes of different fruits or vegetables. Ask one child to close her eyes and identify a particular fruit or vegetable by taste alone.
   b. Talk about favorite and least favorite tastes.
   c. Provide a variety of warm and cold, rough and smooth, or liquid and solid foods (or beverages) to talk about.

5. Discuss the skin and touching.
   a. Find a variety of objects that are different in texture and talk about the way they feel. Discuss objects in the classroom that are rough, smooth, bumpy, hard, soft, silky, and so on.
   b. Talk about things which are pleasant or unpleasant to touch.
   c. Discuss the hot and cold qualities of food and drinks. Which do we like hot and which do we prefer cold?
   d. Show pictures of people living in hot places and cold places. How are they different in their dress? Talk about the way in which the class members change clothing to accompany variations in weather conditions.

Raccoon Mask

1. Have class trace mask.

2. Color mask.

3. Cut out mask. Do not cut out eyes.

4. Using hole puncher, punch holes in mask.

5. Tie 2 lengths of yarn or string to mask through holes.

6. Tie on child.

7. Lead in "blind walk," having parents or older children help.

8. Have children listen and feel and smell and taste.

9. Ask questions about their experience.

NOTE: For Item 15, cut out eyes to use as raccoon mask.

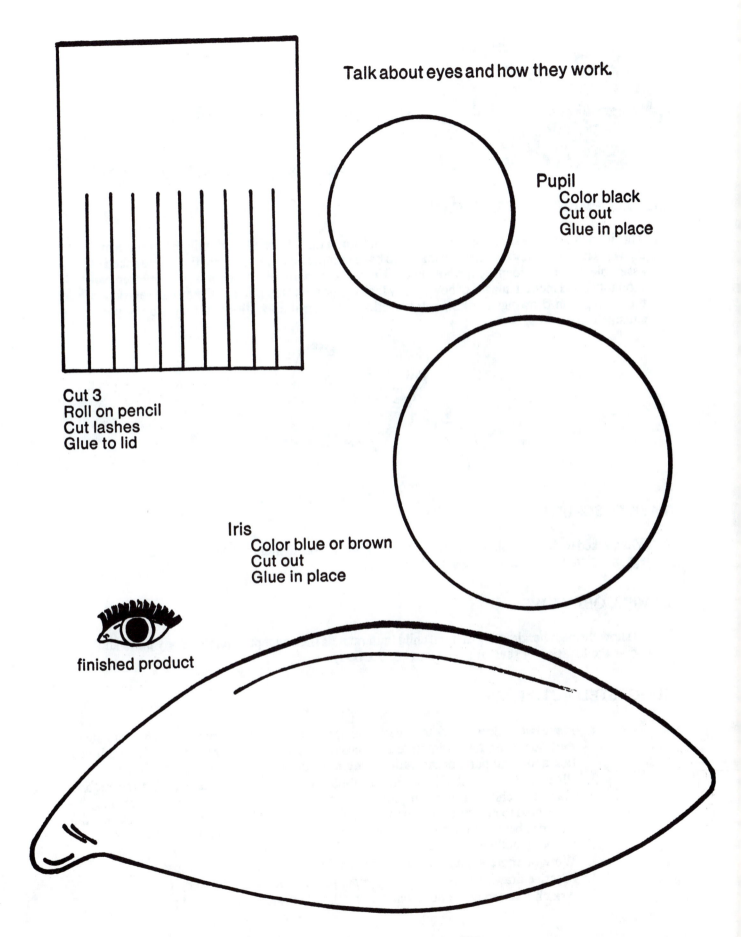

Talk about eyes and how they work.

Pupil
Color black
Cut out
Glue in place

Cut 3
Roll on pencil
Cut lashes
Glue to lid

Iris
Color blue or brown
Cut out
Glue in place

finished product

42 draws a person (I)

Draws a human figure with head, body, arms and legs.

DEVELOPMENTAL SIGNIFICANCE:

This item builds on earlier activities in which children have learned to identify body parts and the ways in which they move. They may also have completed puzzles where they were asked to assemble the pieces to make a whole body. From these manipulative actions the children can probably build mental images of how a body looks. The next step is to see if they can reproduce their images in drawings to show relationships between the locations of major body parts satisfactorily.

TASK DESCRIPTION:

When asked to draw the shape of a person, each child is able to include a head, body, arms, and legs in satisfactory relation to each other.

SAMPLE OBJECTIVE:

To show through her drawing that the child understands the concept of related body parts and knows the location of several major parts of the body.

SUGGESTED ACTIVITIES:

1. Have two children work together. One lies on a large piece of paper which is laid out on the floor. The other attempts to draw around the body with a crayon. Ask the children to talk about the parts of the outline they have drawn.
2. Place an assortment of long colored ribbons on a tray and ask each child to select one. Have the children work in pairs and measure parts of each other. They may be instructed to measure from ear to ear, chin to forehead, and so on. Talk about the differences between the measurements. Complete similar or different measurements on the body outlines created in Activity #1.
3. Work on more sophisticated puzzles dealing with whole body shapes.
4. Practice drawing persons with crayons, pencils, or magic markers.
5. Ask children to name body parts using the illustration on the next page.

 **compares length**

Selects longer of two sticks.

DEVELOPMENTAL SIGNIFICANCE:

Making comparisons and seeking similarities and differences are important elements in effective problem solving. The ability to differentiate a long object from a short object is one element in this process.

TASK DESCRIPTION:

When two sticks are placed next to each other, the child can choose the longer one. The sticks should be the same color and shape.

SAMPLE OBJECTIVE:

To promote problem-solving skills.

SUGGESTED ACTIVITIES:

1. Cut ribbons, pieces of string, lengths of paper or other materials into two pieces. One should be long, the other short. Ask the children to identify which is longer.
2. Collect twigs, weeds or grasses and ask the children to place a long one next to a short one.
3. Look at pictures of animals, fish or birds and compare their body sizes. Alternatively, look at a specific aspect of selected creatures and compare long and short necks, legs, beaks or noses.
4. Makes short and long designs, using the patterns shown on the next page, and ask the children to compare them. The designs may be cut into felt pieces and used on a felt board.
5. In a movement activity, practice walking "tall" and walking "small."

That snake was this long!

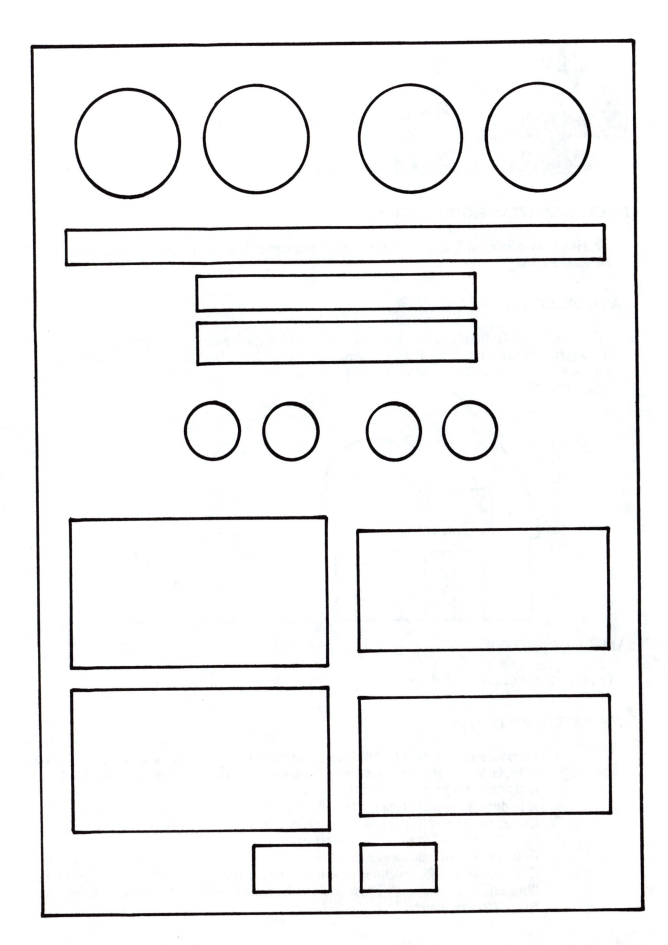

 **compares size**

Selects biggest and smallest from four sizes of balls.

DEVELOPMENTAL SIGNIFICANCE:

This is a more advanced item than #43 in that the child must differentiate between four objects rather than two.

TASK DESCRIPTION:

When four balls of differing size are placed before the child, she is able to select the smallest and the biggest. Blocks, cans, or similar objects may be used instead of balls, but they should all be the same shape and color, differing only in size. The child must know the words "smallest" and "biggest."

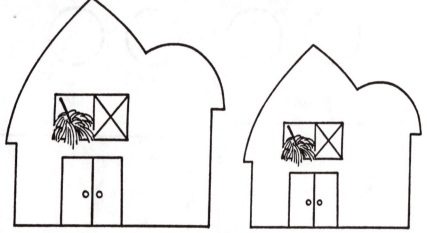

SAMPLE OBJECTIVE:

To promote problem-solving skills.

SUGGESTED ACTIVITIES:

1. Introduce the words "big," "bigger" and "biggest." Compare sets of three toy cars, dolls, beads, crayons or blocks using these words. Let the children play with the objects and practice arranging them in order according to size.
2. Introduce the words "small," "smaller," and "smallest," and repeat Activity #1.
3. Color, cut out and laminate the illustrations shown on the next page. Let the children order them from "smallest" to "biggest."
4. Compare sets of four objects, but focus on the "biggest" and "smallest" in each set.
5. Compare sets of four pictures of similar objects and ask the children to identify the "biggest" and "smallest." These could include pictures of people, animals, mountains, rivers, trees or houses.

Old MacDonald

 **understands numbers (II)**

Understand number concepts to five.

DEVELOPMENTAL SIGNIFICANCE:

This item has the same significance as Item #40 — that is, relating numbers to objects. The ability of a child to understand the concept of "how many" is dependent on her seeing numbers in relations to objects, rather than merely counting by rote. Mastery of this item is indicated when the child is able to readily make the association that specific numbers represent a certain quantity, and that a specific numeral is assigned to each set of objects. Thus, numeral one is given to a set of one object. numeral two is given to a set with two items, and so on. Once this basic foundation has been laid, the child is ready for simple mathematical calculations.

TASK DESCRIPTION:

The child is able to count up to five objects by saying the number word in correspondence to the number of objects placed in a set. The child is able to correctly identify numerals 1-5 and can match numerals 1-5 to number sets.

SAMPLE OBJECTIVE:

To encourage thinking processes.

SUGGESTED ACTIVITIES:

1. Flannel Board Figure Fun.
   Use a flannel board and shapes to show sets containing up to five shapes. Have the children select sets of shapes to place on the board and have them follow with the corresponding numeral. Reverse the activity by allowing children to pick a flannel numeral, then place it next to the correct flannel shape set.
2. Computation Collage.
   Ask each child to pick out a cardboard numeral to trace around and color The cardboard numerals could be covered with varying patterns such as dots, stripes or squares. Let the children cut up old books, magazines, funny papers, etc. and paste to the page as many objects as the numeral that was traced represents. Alternatively, cut out the numeral shapes to use as a body form, and add heads, hands, feet, etc. Hang these from a string so that they move with air currents. The computation collages can be transformed into DANCING DIGITS.
3. "We're Counting On *Us!*" An Activity For Five Year Olds.
   Make a simple body form on a ditto that says "I'm FIVE and FABULOUSLY ALIVE." Have each child select five pictures from books, magazines, etc., that tell about her interests, hobbies, foods, animals, games, family. Cut and paste the pictures on the body form, and then add hair, eyes, and clothes around the pasted pictures. Display the cut-out figures on a board with the caption: "We're Counting on *Us!*"

4. Sort and Eat a Nourishing Number Treat.
   Give each child five small Dixie drink cups which have been numbered from 1-5 with a magic marker. Ask each child to place the corresponding amount of cereal pieces, raisins, or miniature marshmallows in each of her cups. After each child has been "checked off" by the teacher, let her eat her NUMBERS!
5. Sing the song, "Five Little Ducks" using the duck puppets from the following illustration.

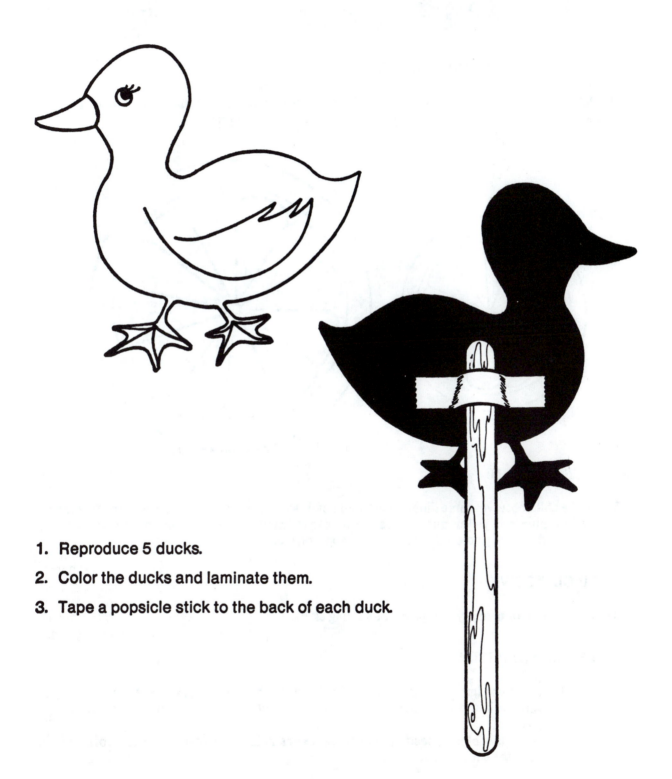

1. Reproduce 5 ducks.

2. Color the ducks and laminate them.

3. Tape a popsicle stick to the back of each duck.

 **detects a pattern**

Copies a pattern based on color, size, or shape in stringing beads or stacking blocks.

DEVELOPMENTAL SIGNIFICANCE:

In detecting and repeating a pattern the child must see it, remember it and then copy it. This behavior is a prerequisite to more advanced intellectual operations.

TASK DESCRIPTION:

When the child observes three different colored beads strung twice in the same sequence (i.e., red, yellow, blue, red, yellow and blue), she is able to repeat the pattern on her own string. The use of three differently colored blocks is also appropriate.

SAMPLE OBJECTIVE:

To develop visual, memory and problem-solving skills.

SUGGESTED ACTIVITIES:

1. Color and laminate the illustrations shown on the next page. Cut them out. Show the children how patterns can be made with them. Let them copy patterns and make up their own.
2. Use sets of blocks, beads, toy cars, leaves or similar items to make patterns of three and have the child repeat them.

Watermelon

Carrot

Orange

understands relative qualities

Demonstrates understanding of relative qualities
in such pairs of words as heavy and light, hot and cold,
and fast and slow.

DEVELOPMENTAL SIGNIFICANCE:

The behaviors required in this item indicate that more advanced thinking is taking place.
Relationships between the qualities of objects are understood. Such understanding generally
requires experience and information beyond the visual or tactile.

TASK DESCRIPTION:

When pictures of objects are shown to the child, he is able to tell which is heavy or light, hot or
cold, and fast or slow. Other meaningful qualities or objects may be substituted.

SAMPLE OBJECTIVE:

To develop thinking skills.

SUGGESTED ACTIVITIES:

1. Use any range of objects or pictures of objects to compare heavy and light, hot and cold,
   or fast and slow. The science experiment shown on the next page illustrates hot and
   cold.
2. In movement classes let the child move heavily and lightly, quickly and slowly, and pretend to be hot or cold.
3. Talk about the use of scales to show heavy and light; thermometers to show hot and
   cold; speedometers to indicate fast or slow.
4. Use the other illustrations shown to discuss other relative qualities.

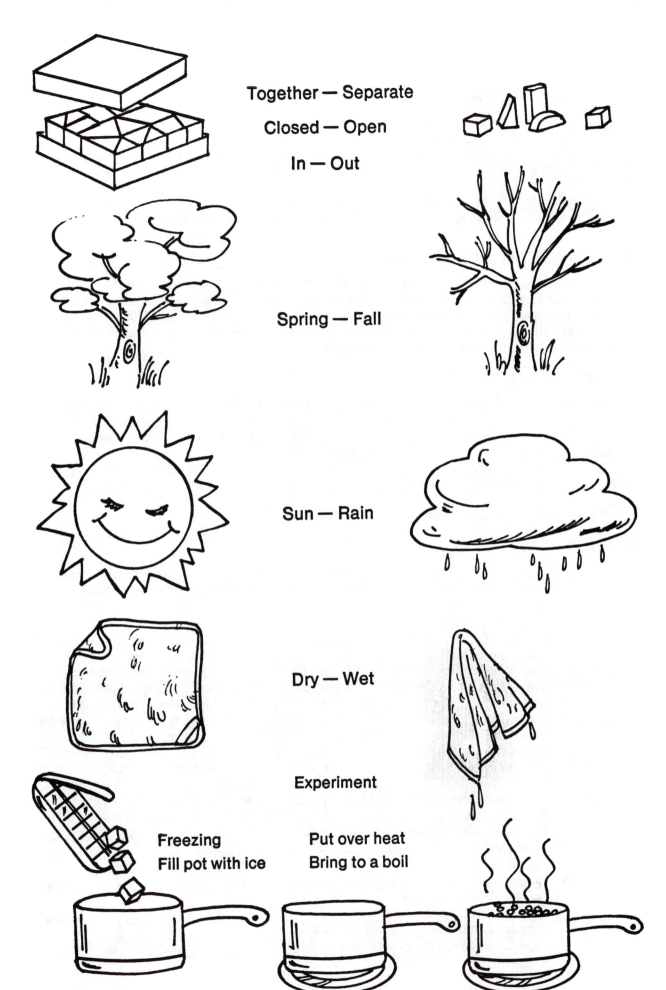

Together — Separate

Closed — Open

In — Out

Spring — Fall

Sun — Rain

Dry — Wet

Experiment

Freezing
Fill pot with ice

Put over heat
Bring to a boil

48 understands numbers (III)

Understands number concepts to ten.

DEVELOPMENTAL SIGNIFICANCE:

This item is a continuation of Items #40 and #45. Its developmental significance is the child's ability to conceptualize higher numbers and to build upon the association that the number of objects perceived is related to an assigned numeral. The development of the child's memory retention skills, as well as associational skills, is necessary for laying a basic foundation upon which future mathematical concepts can be built.

TASK DESCRIPTION:

The child is able to count up to ten objects by saying the number word in correspondence to the quantity of objects placed in a set. The child is able to correctly identify the numerals 6-10 and can match them to number sets. The child is also able to retain the number association for numerals 1-5 which were previously learned in Item #45.

SAMPLE OBJECTIVE:

To encourage thinking processes.

SUGGESTED ACTIVITIES:

1. The activities and games in Items #40 and #45 can be adapted for use with numerals over 5. Once the children have had opportunities for practicing concepts for the higher numerals, combined exercises using numbers 1-10 can be used.

2. Mr. or Ms. Mighty Mathman Maze.
   For this activity, you'll need a "Mighty Mathman" prop and two complete sets of colored beads or blocks. Make a "Mighty Mathman" prop by drawing an eye and mouth on a pizza cardboard (See illustration). Staple a small box to the back of "Mathman" in which to collect the beads or blocks. To play, give each child a different colored bead or block to hold. Put the matching set of beads or blocks in a bag or box to use as the "draw pile." Select one child to be Mr. or Ms. "Mighty Mathman." Have the rest of the children arrange themselves in a "maze" by sitting on the floor (preferably carpeted) of a designated area of the room. Draw or have a child chosen to be "drawer" pick out a bead or block from the draw pile. Mr. or Ms. "Mighty Mathman" must go to the child holding the matching bead and "gobble" it up by putting it in the box stapled to "Mighty Mathman." The child whose bead has been "gobbled" must announce how many total beads have been "gobbled." Continue to draw beads and to count until all the beads or blocks have been "gobbled."

3. Read number books such as *The Counting Book* by Dr. Seuss.

4. Sing number songs such as "Ten Little Indians," "This Old Man . . ." or even "The Twelve Days of Christmas". (This song can be modified to include only ten days. Children can design their own ver-

sions and put their work into a number booklet.)

5. Gone Fishin'.
Using the pattern shown below, cut out ten fish from colored construction paper and number them from 1 to 10. Laminate each fish and slip a paper clip on its mouth. Make a fishing pole with a stick, twine and magnet, as shown. Mark off a "pond" on the floor with masking tape and put all ten fish in the pond. Let the children take turns "fishing" and placing the fish they catch in numerical order.

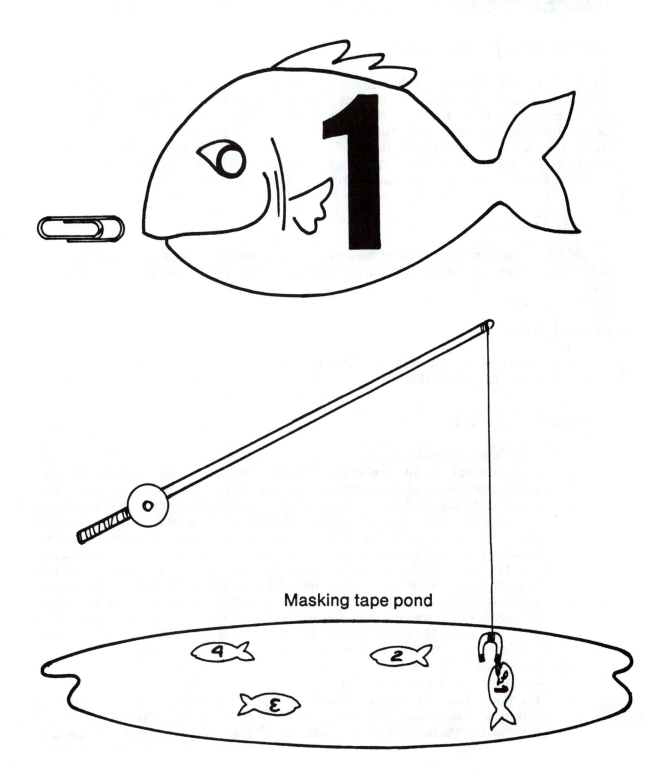

Masking tape pond

knows seasons

Knows seasons of the year and how they relate to events and holidays.
(e.g., "School is out for most of the summer."
"Easter and Passover come in the spring.")

DEVELOPMENTAL SIGNIFICANCE:

Item #32 established that young children are concerned with present-moment experiences which directly affect them. As a child matures, she becomes increasingly aware of concepts beyond simply herself and her immediate environment. Her ability to recognize seasons and to see how they relate to the events in her life, as well as others' lives, is a major indicator that she has a beginning conception of past and future. This capacity to make seasonal associations is necessary if she is to fully comprehend long range consequences of taking responsibility for her behaviors. Decision making and problem solving are dependent on such comprehension.

TASK DESCRIPTION:

The child is able to name the seasons of the year and events and holidays which occur within each season. All meaningful events which are important to the child, family and school can be shared.

SAMPLE OBJECTIVE:

To develop memory skills by making associations.
To encourage problem-solving skills.

SUGGESTED ACTIVITIES:

1. "Suit"able Seasonal Suitcase.
   Pack a real suitcase with clothes that are appropriate for each season of the year. (e.g., gloves, umbrella, sunglasses, snowgoggles, swimsuit, etc.) Make seasonal signs: SUMMER, WINTER, SPRING, FALL, and place them on the floor at intervals. Let each child pull out one item from the suitcase and place it near the appropriate sign. Discuss the idea that some clothes can be worn in one or more seasons, depending on where a person lives in the country.
2. Use a class calendar to emphasize the coming events and holidays. Prepare individual calendar sheets for each child. Color special days or events with certain colors or use words or symbols to emphasize them. For example, Halloween could be colored orange and Columbus Day, blue. Staple the calendars onto a larger piece of paper. Pass the calendars to the children and ask them to decorate the month's calendar appropriately with pictures and colors that represent the events and season.
3. Play Seasonal Charades.
   On small cards, write or draw words or pictures that represent activities which are done in certain seasons. Some suggestions are sledding, swimming, and kite flying. Ask each child to draw out a card, study it then "play act" what they see on the card. The rest of the children must guess what activity and season the actor/actress is trying to represent.

The child who guesses correctly gets to draw out the next card for the others to guess. Continue until all children have had a turn.

4. Use the house activity which follows. Put the child's name next to the word "house" and the name of the season on the next line. Let the children decorate the house in different ways for each season.

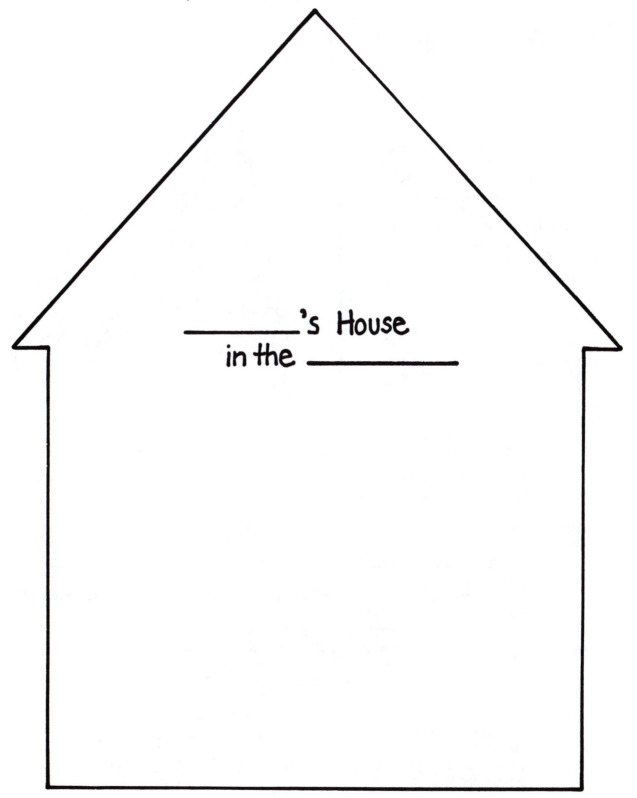

_____'s House
in the _____

50 draws person (II)

Draws human figure with details (fingers, toes, hands, ears, etc.)

DEVELOPMENTAL SIGNIFICANCE:

This item is an elaboration of an earlier item in which children were asked to draw a person showing the major body parts. With reinforcement and practice, language, experience, and memory associated with figures may be expected to increase. Attention to additional details in drawings should accompany these developments.

TASK DESCRIPTION:

When asked to draw the shape of a person, each child should illustrate hands, feet, ears, hair, and similar details in addition to the major body parts.

SAMPLE OBJECTIVE:

To demonstrate that the child understands additional details of body parts and reflects this understanding in her drawing of a person.

SUGGESTED ACTIVITIES:

1. During "rug time" have the children point to particular parts of their bodies and discuss how these look, move, and feel.
2. Introduce the coat hanger skeleton from the next page. Talk about how it is the same or different from a rag doll or a real person. Say the rhyme:
   > I'm walking around in my bones, Ha! Ha!
   > I'm walking around in my bones, Ha! Ha!
   > I took off my skin to let in the light
   > I'm walking around in my bones, Ha! Ha!
3. Use books, songs, and recordings which talk about parts of the body.
4. Cut out pictures of people from magazines and talk with the children about how they are different from each other. Use pictures of faces to show detailed differences between them.
5. Let the children practice drawing figures and discuss with them how they can add further details to their pictures.

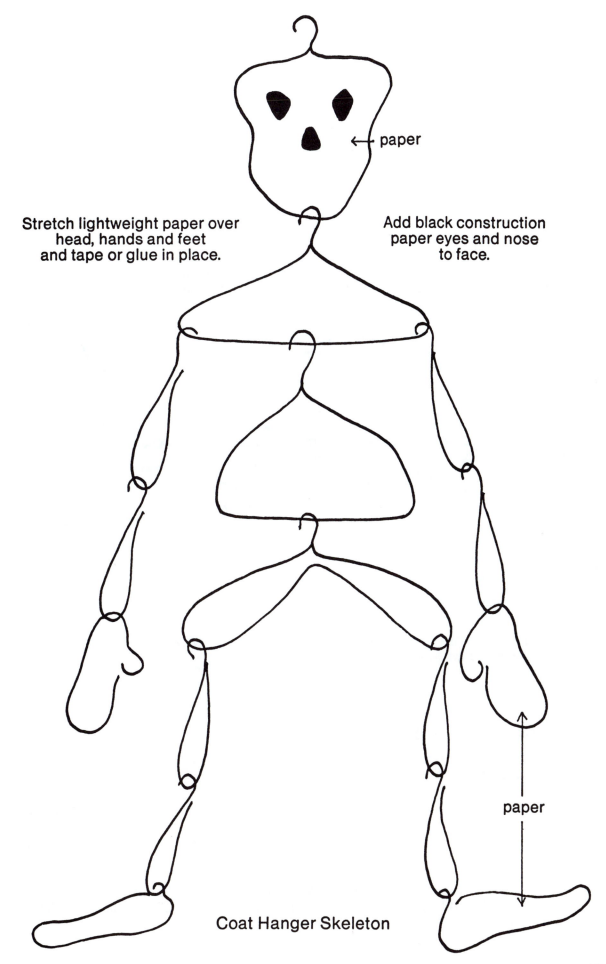

Stretch lightweight paper over head, hands and feet and tape or glue in place.

Add black construction paper eyes and nose to face.

paper

paper

Coat Hanger Skeleton

125

classifies objects (II)

Sorts objects into sets, matching them according to use.

DEVELOPMENTAL SIGNIFICANCE:

This item shows that children's thinking skills and experience have expanded so that they can look at objects from a variety of perspectives and determine one method of classifying them into sets. In this instance the set is based on "use."

TASK DESCRIPTION:

When shown the following six items: a pencil, pen, crayon, knife, fork and spoon, the child is able to sort them into two sets, based on their use.

SAMPLE OBJECTIVE:

To encourage thinking, classifying and problem-solving skills.

SUGGESTED ACTIVITIES:

1. Show children sets of objects such as china, clothing and toys. Mix the objects up and ask the group to sort them out into the correct set according to use.
2. Talk about special places where sets of special things are kept together. Books in the library, animals at the zoo and food at the supermarket are examples.
3. Use the columns on the following page and ask the children to find pictures of people or creatures using the air, water or land. Paste the pictures in the appropriate column. If desired, start by showing children the illustration on page 128 and ask the children to classify the means of transportation by air, water or land.

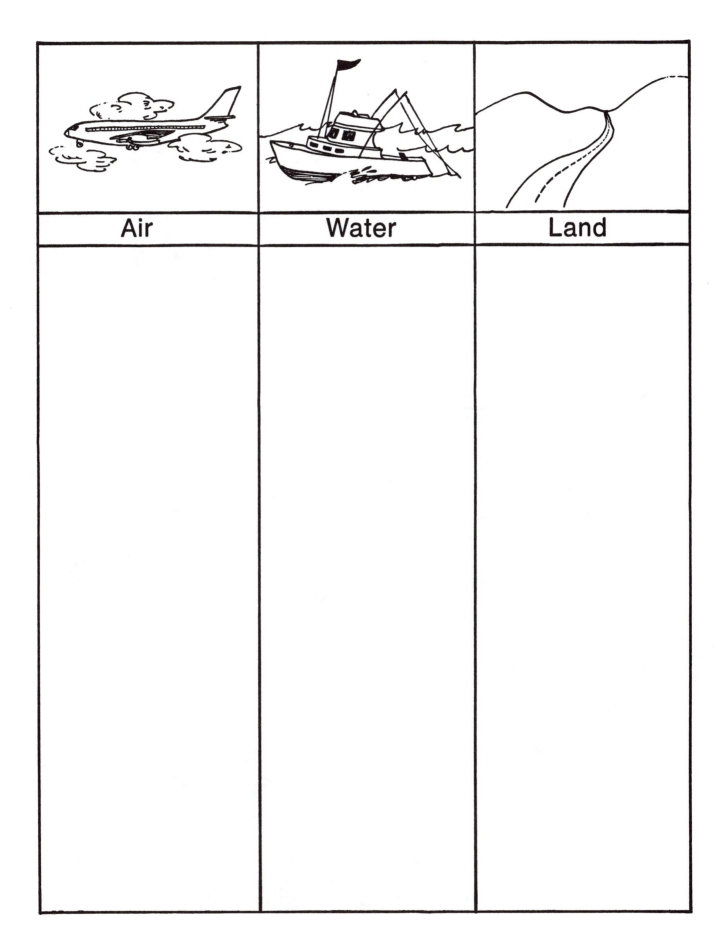

Air	Water	Land

recognizes fantasy

Distinguishes between fantasy and reality.

DEVELOPMENTAL SIGNIFICANCE:

The very young child can not easily differentiate between what is real and what is make-believe. Sometimes television movie stars, as well as storybook heroes and heroines, are as alive and real to her as members of her family and next door neighbors. Although fantasy and imagination are cherished parts of childhood, it is important that the child be able to recognize what is real and what is unreal. The ability of a child to deal with reality while giving fantasy an important place in her life, however, indicates that she is developing higher-level skills.

TASK DESCRIPTION:

The child is able to tell whether a situation is real or make-believe when confronted with examples in a variety of formats such as books, movies, filmstrips, play acting, personal dilemmas, etc. The child shows appreciation for and enjoyment in her ability to pretend and make-believe, and understands those times in which its use is appropriate behavior.

SAMPLE OBJECTIVE:

To encourage thinking processes.
To develop problem-solving skills.

SUGGESTED ACTIVITIES:

1. Read books that deal with make-believe. Some suggestions are: *The Mango Tooth* by Charlotte Pomerantz; *My Friend, Jasper Jones* by Rosamond Dauer; or *Every Day A Dragon* by Joan M. Lexau. All books are suitable for children ages 3-7.

2. Show several animated cartoon filmstrips. Tall tales, such as *Paul Bunyan and His Blue Ox* or *Pecos Bill* are particularly good since, in addition to having make-believe cartoon characters, the story line is extremely distorted. Discuss how this filmstrip contains fantasy. In comparison, show children a good nature film. (All Walt Disney nature films are excellent.) Discuss how this film is real. As an extension activity, try to find a film or movie that is a combination of fantasy and reality. *Dot and The Kangaroo* or *Song of the South* are two movies that have elements of both what is real and what is unreal.

3. Discuss the "Superheroes" that are popular on television and in books. Let each child draw a picture about her favorite hero and tell why she likes this make-believe character. If time allows, let each child dress-up, using masks or costumes, and pretend that she is a superhero. Build the emphasis of this activity around the idea that it is fun to pretend and to play dress-up but that "Super Me" is neater — and real!

4. The Cat Did It!
   Talk with children about some things that they have done which got them into trouble.

Make a general list of personal dilemmas. Tell a story about a little girl named Fantasia and incorporate the children's list of troubles into the storyline. Whenever Fantasia gets into trouble, however, she always says: "The cat did it!" Let the children help with the story by saying this line in unison each time Fantasia says it in the story. At the end, finish the story by asking the children, "Did the cat *really* do all those things?" The children should be able to recognize that the story character used fantasy to avoid dealing with her own actions. Help children to realize that each of us is responsible for our own behaviors.

5. It's The Real Thing!
    Cook in the classroom using realistic recipes. Use simple ingredients that children can measure and mix. Apple salad or celery sticks stuffed with peanut butter are both nutritious and easy. As an extension of this activity, ask the children to create and draw a fantasy recipe. For example, "Fantasy Fudge" could be made of chocolate moon creatures and meteorites, laced with Martian marshmallows. It would be "out of this world."

6. Help the children find and cut out pictures of real animals. Let them tell you about their natural habitat, eating habits, etc. Then have the children make the paper plate animal puppets like those shown and pretend with them. Let the children make up stories about their puppets and act them out with the puppets.

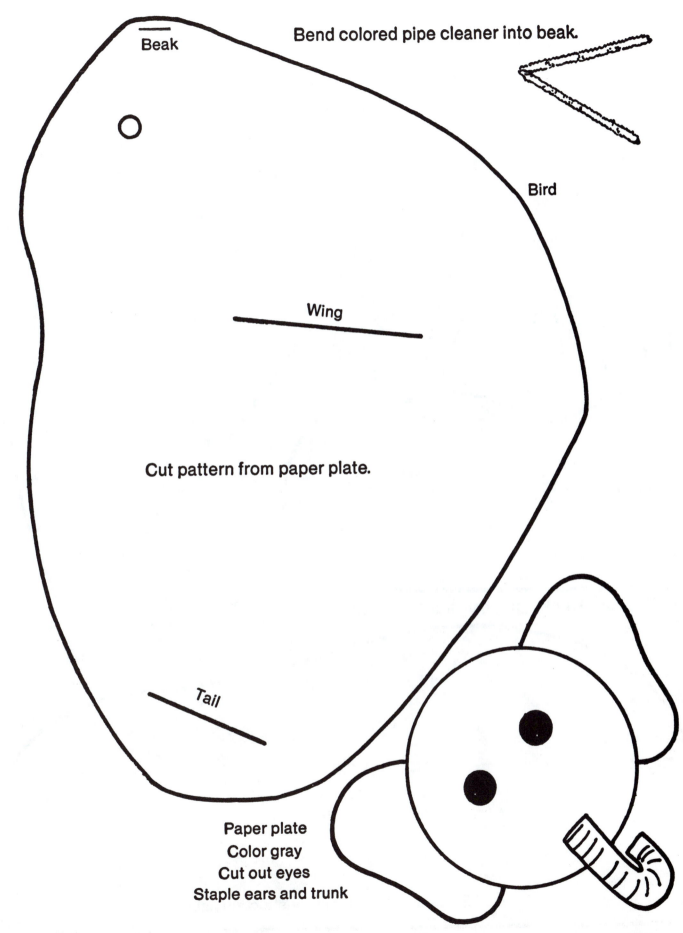

Beak

Bend colored pipe cleaner into beak.

Bird

Wing

Cut pattern from paper plate.

Tail

Paper plate
Color gray
Cut out eyes
Staple ears and trunk

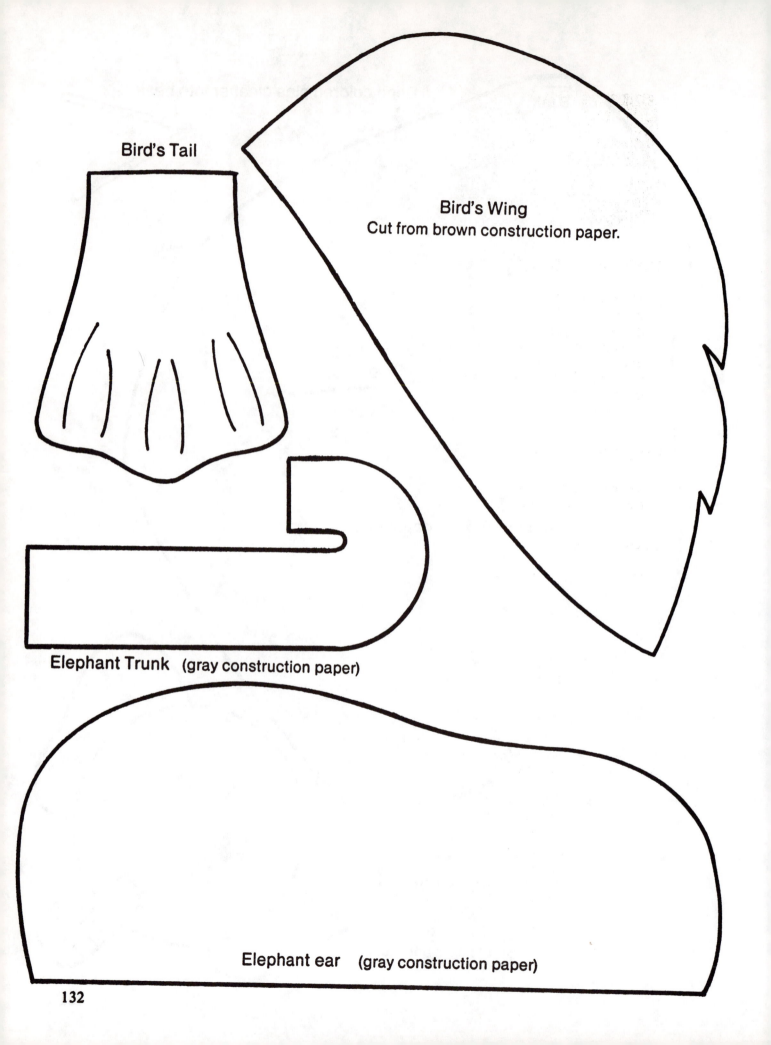

Bird's Tail

Bird's Wing
Cut from brown construction paper.

Elephant Trunk   (gray construction paper)

Elephant ear   (gray construction paper)

132

recognizes cause and effect

Shows awareness of the relationship between an action and its cause.

DEVELOPMENTAL SIGNIFICANCE:

The young child becomes increasingly aware of her environment through her experiences. As she explores and discovers new and exciting things, she becomes interested in "how" or "why" things happen. She is curious about her world, and her increasing curiosity causes her to be less accepting of things she sees or hears. She needs further explanation to understand and gain control over her environment. She feels more secure knowing that things happen as a result of other things and that there is a relationship between an action and its cause. Her ability to conceptualize this idea will enable her to use problem-solving skills in coping with her expanding environment.

TASK DESCRIPTION:

The child demonstrates an awareness of the relationship between an action (water boils) and its cause (heat is applied).

SAMPLE OBJECTIVE:

To encourage problem-solving skills.

SUGGESTED ACTIVITIES:

1. The Mystery Man Strikes Again — Or Has He?
   Before children are assembled for this activity, set up a table with a painted picture, spilled water, a half-eaten cookie, modeled clay, and a stack of blocks. (Substitutions can be made according to what is convenient in the classroom). As the children come into the room, announce, "The mystery man strikes again — or has he?" Ask children if they can tell you what happened *before*, using what was left behind on the table. What *caused* each thing? As an extension of this activity, allow children to take turns being the Mystery Man by placing something on the table that their actions have caused or by manipulating objects to create an effect or situation, while the other children hide their eyes. Let the other children guess what the Mystery Man did to cause what has appeared on the table.

2. Green Eggs and Ham.
   Fry eggs in the classroom to let children watch the changes the eggs undergo as heat is applied to them. If desired, read *Green Eggs and Ham* by Dr. Seuss to the children first, and then add green food coloring to the eggs as you cook them. Let the children enjoy eating those funny-looking green eggs! As a follow-up activity, make the egg and frying pan from the pattern on the next page. If children desire, they may color the egg green.

"Cooking eggs, color them green, funniest thing I've ever seen."

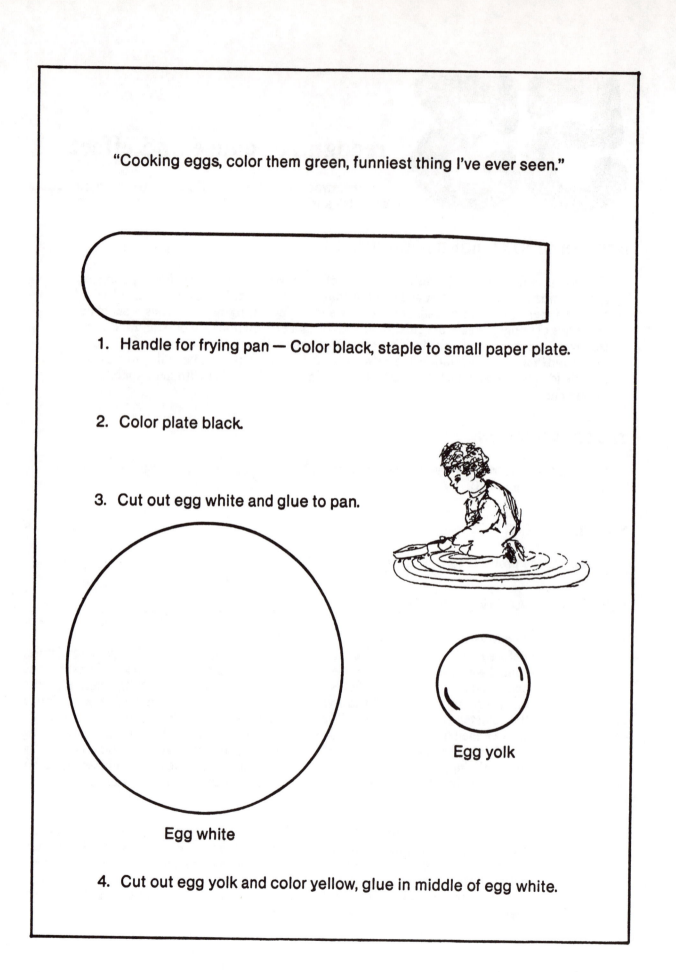

1. Handle for frying pan — Color black, staple to small paper plate.

2. Color plate black.

3. Cut out egg white and glue to pan.

Egg yolk

Egg white

4. Cut out egg yolk and color yellow, glue in middle of egg white.

 # predicts outcome

Anticipates the consequences of simple actions.

DEVELOPMENTAL SIGNIFICANCE:

In Item #53, the child has become aware of the effect that actions have on situations. Once the child understands that some things happen as a result of other actions, she will be able to predict the outcome of a situation. The child is making logical associations if she can comprehend that touching a hot flame will burn her hand or that picking up the telephone receiver will stop the telephone from ringing. Her expanding memory skills and developing thought processes allow her to rationalize the outcome of many situations. This ability to think through a situation before acting will increase her capacity to cope with a variety of experiences in her broadening environment.

TASK DESCRIPTION:

The child is able to tell what will happen next when confronted with a simple action. (e.g., the child will be able to predict that pushing the button on the door will cause the doorbell to ring).

SAMPLE OBJECTIVE:

To develop memory skills.
To encourage problem-solving skills.

SUGGESTED ACTIVITIES:

1. Refer to activities that are related to sequencing skills. Items #16 and #28 are appropriate to use.
2. Read the story, *Herbie's Troubles* by Chapman. This is a delightful story about a boy's problems with another student. The story-line is recurring so that the outcome is predictable. The children can "tell" these predictable parts as the teacher comes to them. The ending is different, so it would be fun to see who is perceptive enough to figure it out.
3. Do an experiment called: PREDICTING PLANTS POSES PUZZLES.
Plant three cups of beans with equal amounts of soil, water and seeds. Give one plant light and water, the second water, and the third only light. Let the children predict what will happen to each one.

Chapter 6

Humanics National Child Assessment Form: Motor Skills Development

ITEMS 55-72

**55** walks on tip toes

Can walk on tip toes for four to five steps.

DEVELOPMENTAL SIGNIFICANCE:

The ability to walk on tip toes shows that the child is developing increased bodily control and focus on a specific part of the body.

TASK DESCRIPTION:

Following a direction from the teacher, the child walks on tip toe for three or four steps.

SAMPLE OBJECTIVE:

To develop gross motor coordination.

SUGGESTED ACTIVITIES:

1. Show the children how they have to stand on tip toe to reach tall objects.
2. Show how walking on tiptoe is used to demonstrate "quiet walking."
3. Let the children tiptoe around the room to quiet music.
4. Practice any reaching activity. For example, pretend to reach for a star.

Reach for the stars.
Use stars from Activity #4.

56 walks balance board

Walks a balance board 6" wide, 3" off the ground.

DEVELOPMENTAL SIGNIFICANCE:

Balance is an important part of bodily control. The ability to balance increases self-confidence.

TASK DESCRIPTION:

Place a board of approximately five feet in length and six inches in width about three inches off the ground. See if the child can walk across the board without falling off.

SAMPLE OBJECTIVE:

To develop gross motor coordination.

SUGGESTED ACTIVITIES:

1. Tape two parallel lines of tape to the floor about eight inches apart. Let the children practice walking between them.
2. Play "Follow the Leader" activities using a chalk line on the playground, a railroad tie, a log or a curb, as a practice activity.
3. Let children be "Tin Can High Walkers." Make tin can "stilts" as directed on the following illustration. Show the class how to balance on the cans holding the ropes tightly in their hands. When the children are comfortable standing on the cans, suggest that they walk around a table or across a rug. Further suggestion: When doing a circus unit, use the "Tin Can High Walkers" as an act.

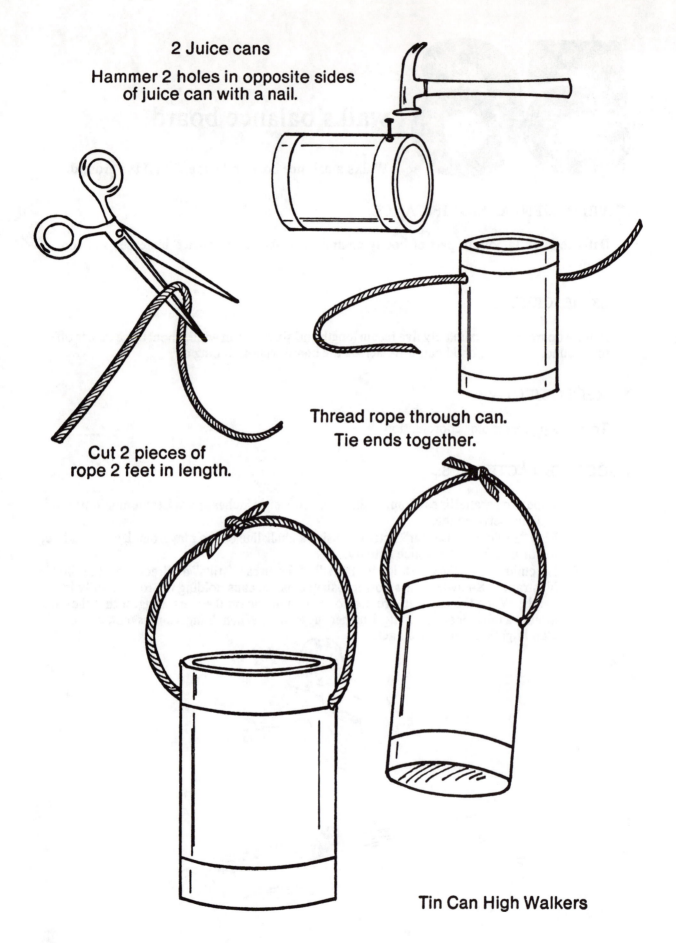

2 Juice cans

Hammer 2 holes in opposite sides of juice can with a nail.

Cut 2 pieces of rope 2 feet in length.

Thread rope through can. Tie ends together.

Tin Can High Walkers

jumps from stool

Jumps from 12" high object without falling.

DEVELOPMENTAL SIGNIFICANCE:

This item is an indication of increasing body control. It also helps children understand certain concepts, including "off" and "on."

TASK DESCRIPTION:

The child is able to jump off an object which is approximately 12" high without falling.

SAMPLE OBJECTIVE:

To develop gross motor skills.

SUGGESTED ACTIVITIES:

1. Have the children jump off boxes or other objects of increasing heights.
2. Let children play "Ringmaster," taking turns standing on the Ringmaster's "block" to announce circus acts. (See illustration on next page.) Children will also enjoy jumping on and off the block as part of their Ringmaster play.

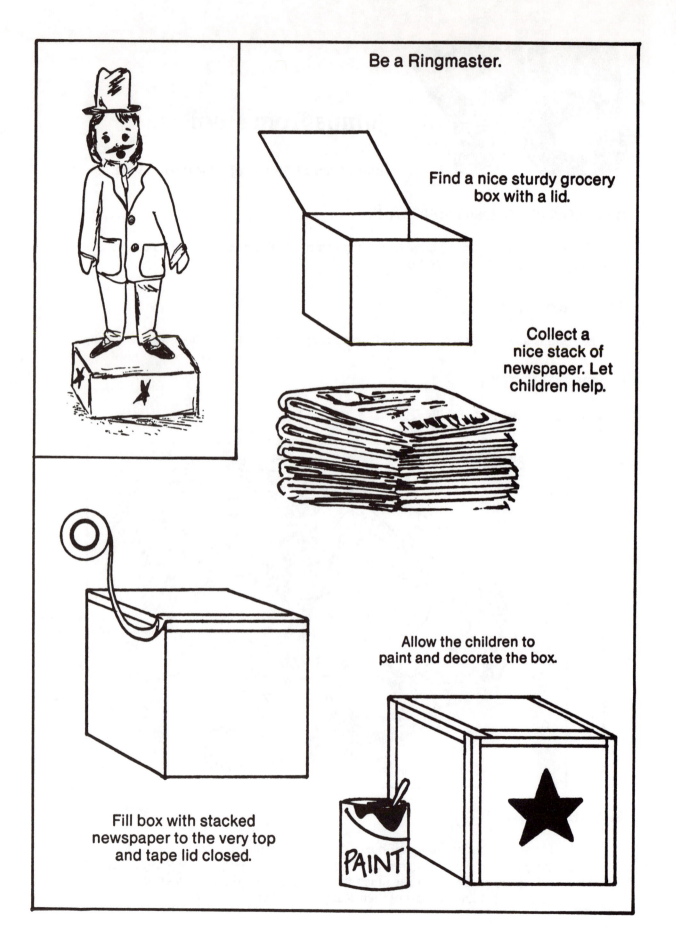

Be a Ringmaster.

Find a nice sturdy grocery box with a lid.

Collect a nice stack of newspaper. Let children help.

Allow the children to paint and decorate the box.

Fill box with stacked newspaper to the very top and tape lid closed.

PAINT

58

hops on one foot

Hops on one foot at least three times in succession.

DEVELOPMENTAL SIGNIFICANCE:

Hopping activities involve both balance and an awareness of "right" and "left". The child's increasing leg strength is indicated by her ability to balance on one foot or the other.

TASK DESCRIPTION:

The child is able to hop on the right foot and the left foot for three successive hops without losing balance.

SAMPLE OBJECTIVE:

To develop gross motor skills.

SUGGESTED ACTIVITIES:

1. Have children practice standing on the left foot and then the right foot.
2. Have children practice hopping on one foot and then the other.
3. Have children play "Hop Scotch Hill."

Hop Scotch Hill

Find an old shower curtain liner or a long piece of wrapping paper. If necessary, cut off holes. With permanent markers, make a colorful course for the children to hop.

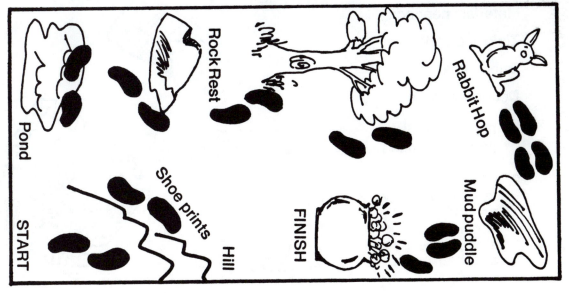

59

catches ball (I)

Catches bounced ball of 12" diameter in arms.

DEVELOPMENTAL SIGNIFICANCE:

This skill requires understanding of space, shape and distance, and eye-hand coordination.

TASK DESCRIPTION:

The child is able to catch a large ball in two hands and arms when it is bounced towards her.

SAMPLE OBJECTIVE:

To develop eye-hand coordination in conjunction with gross motor skills.

SUGGESTED ACTIVITIES:

1. Have children play with bean bags, using one of the many good bean bag activity records. (See following illustration for an easy-to-make bean bag.)
2. Place the children in a group. Have the children pass a large ball from one to another using both hands.
3. Throw the ball to each child in turn. The children try to catch the ball with two hands.
4. Bounce the ball to each child in turn. The children try to catch the ball with two hands.

Bean Bag

Materials needed:

Ziplock plastic bag

Dried peas

Decorative tape

1. Fill ziplock plastic bags with dried peas.
2. Close bag and tape all the way around, lapping half of tape on one side of the bag and half on the other.

60 throws ball

Throws 3" ball in generally intended direction.

DEVELOPMENTAL SIGNIFICANCE:

This item indicates increasing eye-hand coordination and understanding of spatial relationships. It requires the child to control the direction in which a ball is aimed.

TASK DESCRIPTION:

The child is able to aim the ball in a specified direction.

SAMPLE OBJECTIVE:

To develop gross motor skills with increasing concentration on eye-hand coordination.

SUGGESTED ACTIVITIES:

1. As a prerequisite, play the "Soda Bottle Bowling Game." Collect five liter soda bottles. Wrap the center of each bottle with colored construction paper. Create a bowling alley on the floor with two parallel strips of masking tape. Mark the placement for the soda bottle pins with masking tape X's. Start the game with a large ball and a short lane. As the children improve, use smaller balls and a longer alley.
2. After rolling activities, have children practice throwing the ball.
3. Place the children in a circle. Stand in the center of the circle and have the children practice throwing the ball to you.

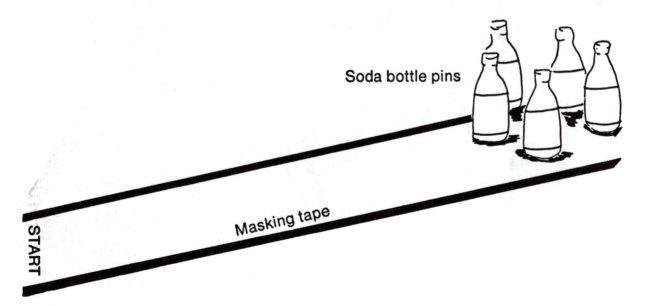

Soda bottle pins

Masking tape

START

61 balances on one foot

Balances on one foot for a slow count of three.

DEVELOPMENTAL SIGNIFICANCE:

Standing on one foot requires a good sense of balance, confidence and coordination.

TASK DESCRIPTION:

The child is able to balance on one foot for a slow count of three seconds.

SAMPLE OBJECTIVE:

To develop gross motor skills.

SUGGESTED ACTIVITIES:

1. Have the children raise one leg to a count of three. Then raise the other leg to a similar count.
2. Have the children play "Mr. Clown." Make the Mr. Clown hat shown on the next page. Place the hat on one child's head and give Mr. (Ms.) Clown directions: "Mr. Clown stand on one foot. Mr. Clown stand on the other foot," and so forth. Let the children take turns being Mr./Ms. Clown.
3. Have children play "Hop Scotch Hill" from Item 58.

Mr. Clown Hat

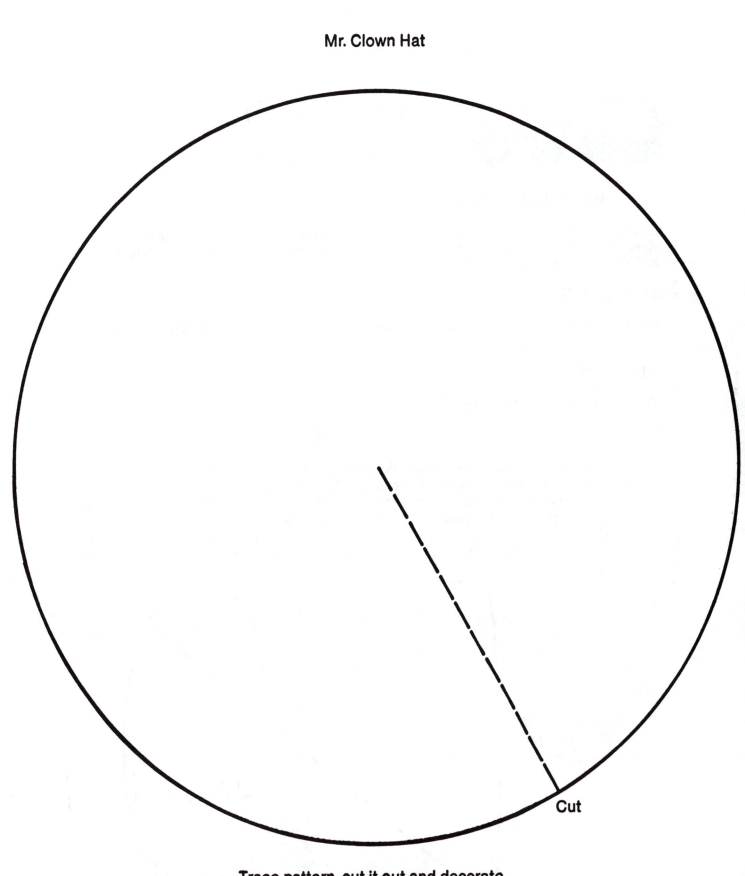

Cut

Trace pattern, cut it out and decorate.
Staple the hat into a cone. Place hat on child's head.

 **works puzzle (I)**

Can put together a three-piece puzzle.

DEVELOPMENTAL SIGNIFICANCE:

Children need to recognize when objects are made up of several pieces. From observing an entire object, they should be able to reconstruct it when shown the two or three pieces which compose it. This is a problem-solving skill.

TASK DESCRIPTION:

When shown two three-piece puzzles which are exactly the same, the child is able to reconstruct one to match the other.

SAMPLE OBJECTIVE:

To promote problem-solving skills.

SUGGESTED ACTIVITIES:

1. Cut a picture in half. Discuss how the two pieces fit together.
2. Cut a picture into three parts. Have the children reassemble it.
3. Make each child a peanut butter sandwich or have each child make her own. When each child has a sandwich, have the children cut their sandwiches into three parts and separate the pieces. Then have the children push their "puzzle" pieces together to reform the sandwich, and eat it. As an alternative, use the peanut butter sandwich puzzle pattern shown.

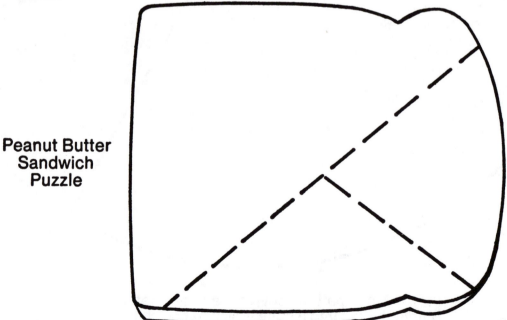

**Peanut Butter
Sandwich
Puzzle**

copies a circle and a cross

Copies a circle, drawing a single line and returning to a general point of beginning. Copies a cross.

DEVELOPMENTAL SIGNIFICANCE:

The ability to copy a circle requires good eye-hand coordination and illustrates understanding of this geometric shape. Similar coordination is required to complete a cross.

TASK DESCRIPTION:

Having been shown how to make a circle and a cross, the child successfully copies each figure.

SAMPLE OBJECTIVE:

To develop a fine motor coordination.

SUGGESTED ACTIVITIES:

1. Show the child the shape of a circle. Let her draw similar shapes. If desired, treat her drawings as "balloons" which she can then color in.
2. Show the child how to make a cross. Let her draw similar ones.
3. Have the children complete the activity sheets which follow. For Activity Sheet I, have the children start with the solid circles on the first row. Instruct the children to trace the first circle in the row with a crayon and then to continue by making increasingly smaller concentric circles within the printed circle until it is completely colored in. Have the children repeat this action with the rest of the solid circles on that row and then move onto the circles drawn with a broken line on the next row. Then have them repeat this activity on the circles shown in the third row. In the fourth row, have children draw their own circles and color them in in the same manner.

   For Activity Sheet II, starting with row one, instruct the children to trace the solid vertical lines, from top to bottom, one at a time. On row two, have the children trace the first vertical line from top to bottom, then trace the horizontal line which crosses it from left to right (as if they were making a "t"), then move onto the next vertical line, etc. Have the children continue to make "t's" or crosses in the same manner on the third and fourth rows.

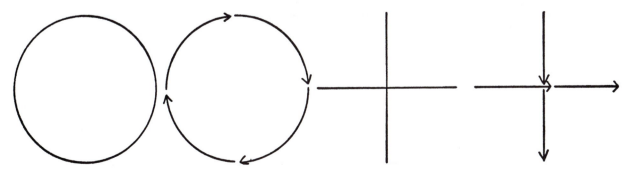

ACTIVITY SHEET I

ACTIVITY SHEET II

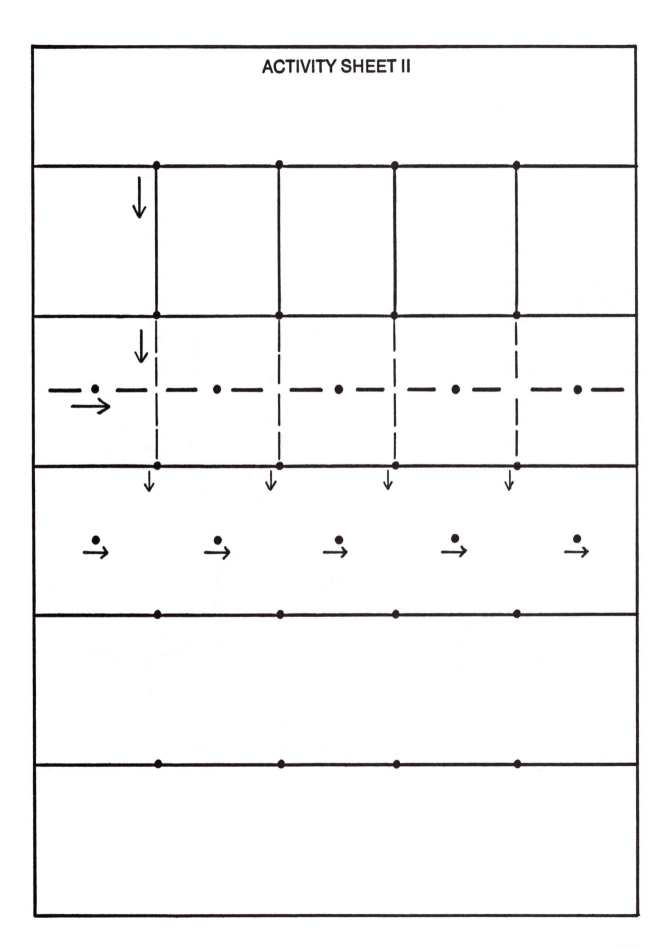

 **gallops**

Gallops continuously for a limited distance.

DEVELOPMENTAL SIGNIFICANCE:

The ability to gallop is a further indication of growing agility, coordination and rhythm. To gallop, the child must display good body control and be able to maintain a simple pattern of movement.

TASK DESCRIPTION:

The child is able to gallop, keeping one foot ahead of the other, for a short distance. Ten to twelve feet is sufficient.

SAMPLE OBJECTIVE:

To develop a rhythmic pattern using gross motor skills.

SUGGESTED ACTIVITIES:

1. To practice galloping, have the children lead with one foot and then bring the other foot up next to it. Encourage them to increase their pace. Use galloping music to accompany this activity.
2. Make the circus hobby horse shown in the accompanying illustration. Let the children practice galloping with it.

"I'm the cowgirl for the circus!
I gallop round and round the ring!"

CIRCUS HORSE

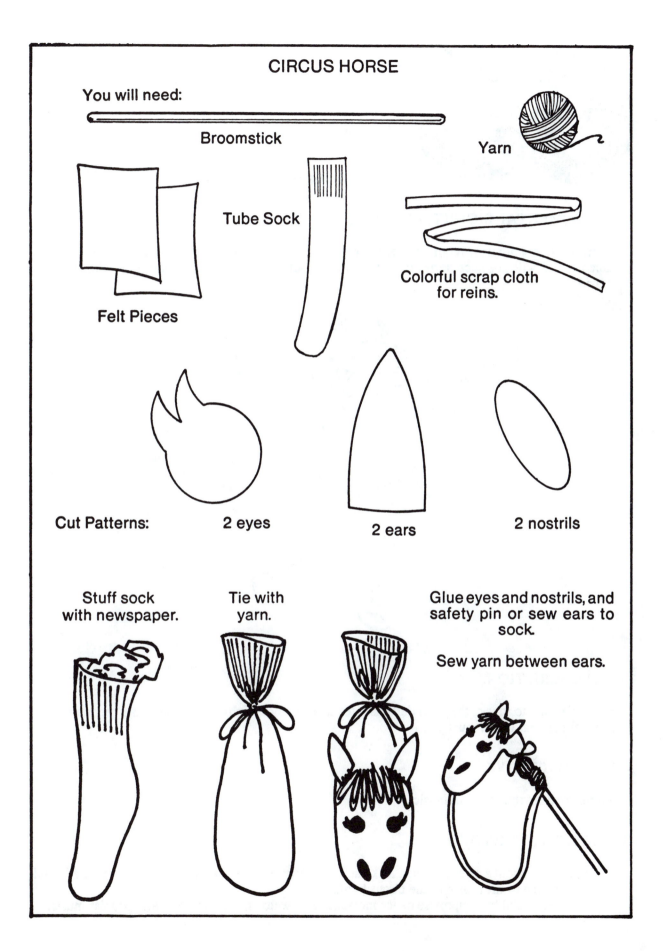

You will need:

Broomstick

Yarn

Felt Pieces

Tube Sock

Colorful scrap cloth for reins.

Cut Patterns:

2 eyes

2 ears

2 nostrils

Stuff sock with newspaper.

Tie with yarn.

Glue eyes and nostrils, and safety pin or sew ears to sock.

Sew yarn between ears.

65 dances

Dances with a sense of rhythm.

DEVELOPMENTAL SIGNIFICANCE:

Dancing, like galloping, requires overall control of the body. Movements should be spontaneous and will not necessarily follow a pattern, but they should be in harmony with the music.

TASK DESCRIPTION:

While dancing to music, the child demonstrates a semblance of rhythm. Movements generally parallel the beat of the music.

SAMPLE OBJECTIVE:

To respond rhythmically to music.

SUGGESTED ACTIVITIES:

1. Talk about a circus parade. Ask each child to pretend to be a performer in the parade and dance to the music of the circus band.
2. Have children improvise dance movements to waltzes, marches, folk and popular music.

explores space

Explores space by moving in several directions.

DEVELOPMENTAL SIGNIFICANCE:

The exploration of space is an important element in movement activities. Changing the direction of a pattern or sequence of actions includes turning around, going sideways or moving backwards.

TASK DESCRIPTION:

During movement activities, the child explores space by changing directions.

SUGGESTED ACTIVITIES:

1. Let the children sit on the floor with a good space between them. Ask them to practice "growing up tall and sitting down small."
2. Call on two children to exchange spaces with each other as quickly as they can. Then change the tempo of the game and increase the number of players.
3. Have children make the space helmets shown below and wear the helmets while pretending to be space explorers walking in space or on the moon. Have the children move in slow motion and practice the exaggerated movements associated with weightlessness.

Space Helmets

Draw opening
large enough for a
child's face in medium-
sized paper bag.

Allow children to
cut out hole.

Have children decorate
bags to look like
space helmets.

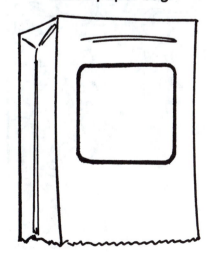
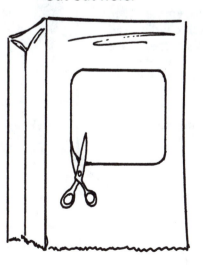
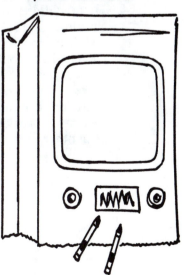

works puzzle (II)

Can successfully assemble a simple five-piece puzzle.

DEVELOPMENTAL SIGNIFICANCE:

The child displays both problem-solving skills and fine motor coordination when she is able to take apart and reassemble a five-piece puzzle, matching a copy.

TASK DESCRIPTION:

The child reconstructs a five-piece puzzle made of wood or other thick material.

SAMPLE OBJECTIVE:

To promote problem-solving strategies and fine motor coordination.

SUGGESTED ACTIVITIES:

1. Ensure that the child is successful with less complicated puzzles (Item #62) before providing her with five-piece puzzles.
2. Give the child a completed five-piece puzzle. Ask her to take it apart and reassemble it correctly from an illustration of the whole picture.
3. Obtain carpet squares from your local decorating center. With a matte knife, create a five-piece carpet puzzle from each square (see illustration). Have children reassemble these carpet puzzles.
4. Have children reassemble "Me Puzzles." Trace each child's head and shoulders on butcher paper. Have each child cut out her own outline and cut the bust into five pieces to make a puzzle of herself. (See illustration on the next page.) Let children swap puzzles and reassemble each other.

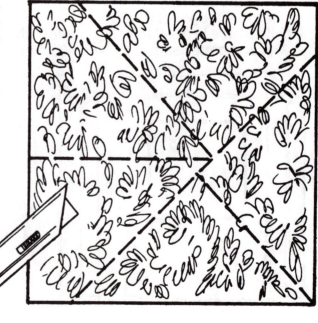

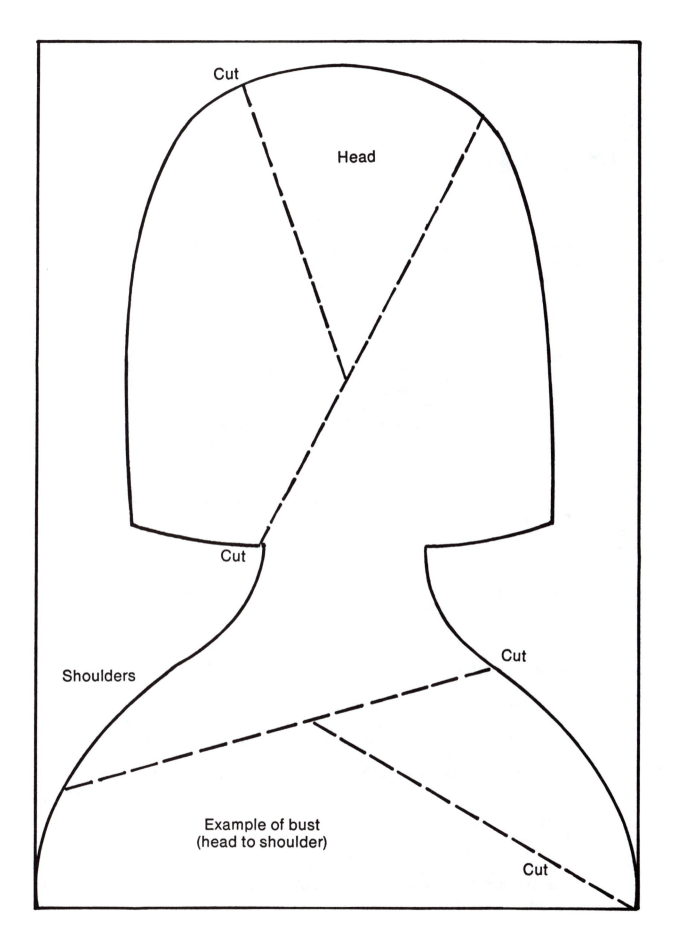

Cut

Head

Cut

Shoulders

Cut

Example of bust
(head to shoulder)

Cut

uses scissors

Uses scissors smoothly and with moderate control; cuts on a drawn line.

DEVELOPMENTAL SIGNIFICANCE:

Using scissors requires fine-motor coordination. Control over the implement shows increasing dexterity with fingers.

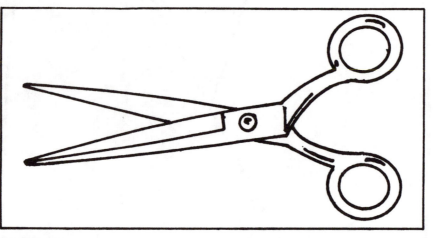

TASK DESCRIPTION:

The child is able to hold a pair of scissors with sufficient skill to cut into a piece of paper.

SAMPLE OBJECTIVE:

To refine fine-motor skills.

SUGGESTED ACTIVITIES:

1. Have children practice tearing pieces of waste paper.
2. Allow the children to cut the edge of a piece of paper to make an irregular figure.
3. Let the children cut out their own shapes. Glue these onto a piece of construction paper to make *mosaic* pictures.
4. Start with paper of narrow width. Fold pieces of this paper in half and open them up again. On other sheets, draw a line across the width of the paper. Have the children cut the paper in half along the folds and along the lines. As the children's dexterity improves, use papers of greater widths, gradually increasing the length of folds and lines to be cut.
5. Have each child do the Spiral Snake activity which follows. Give each child a copy of the Spiral Snake pattern. Instruct the children about using scissors on curves and then have the children cut along the solid lines. Punch a hole for the snake's mouth and tie a 6" piece of yarn through the hole. Holding the free end of the yarn, show each child the spiral she's made with her cutting.

Mr. Spiral Snake

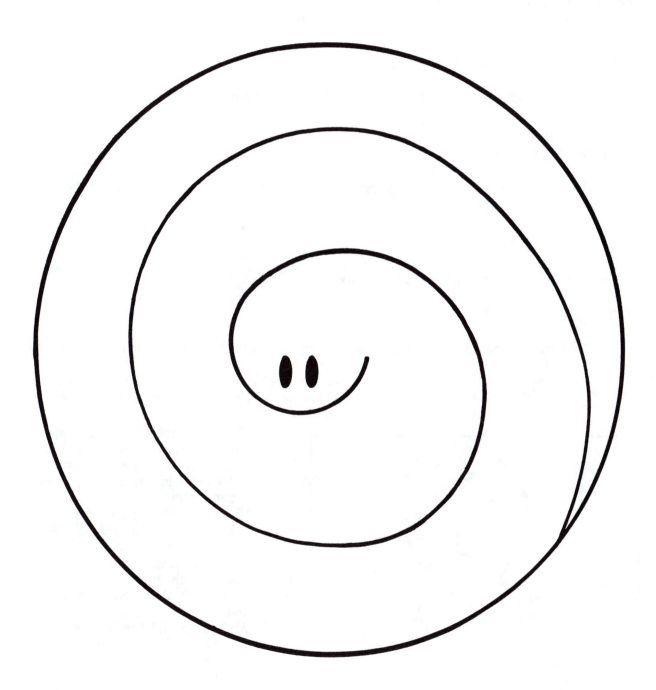

**69** copies letters

Copies large capital letters.

DEVELOPMENTAL SIGNIFICANCE:

The ability to copy upper case letters is a pre-writing and pre-reading activity. It builds on Item #34.

TASK DESCRIPTION:

After being shown how to construct an upper case letter with play dough or other materials, the child is able to copy the shape.

SAMPLE OBJECTIVE:

To learn capital letters as a fine-motor activity.

SUGGESTED ACTIVITIES:

1. Play alphabet games and sing alphabet songs. Point to the letters of the alphabet while doing these activities.
2. Using labels already in place in the classroom, book jackets, advertisements in magazines or product labels, have the children point to the capital letters. Call out the letters by name and have the children point to them in response.

3. Cut out shapes of capital letters from cardboard or other materials and let the children feel them, color them in and possibly draw around them.
4. Show the children how the make their initials with play dough. Follow the recipe given in Item #34.
5. Continue Suggested Activity #4 until the children have practiced making all the upper case letter shapes.
6. Make a Special Touch Typewriter for the children to play and experiment with. (See illustration on next page.) Have the children write one line of one letter on a piece of paper. Put this paper in the typewriter when the children pretend to type.

Special Touch Typewriter

1. Cut a soapbox as shown. Discard top half.

2. Flip bottom half of box over so that open area rests on table or other work surface. Cut out top of typewriter as shown. Paint typewriter red.

3. Cut 26 circles the same size and write letters of the alphabet on circles.

4. Paint cardboard tube black or cover with black construction paper.

5. Paint tube on top of typewriter and glue "keys" to front.

skips

Skips continuously for a defined distance.

DEVELOPMENTAL SIGNIFICANCE:

Skipping is a more sophisticated development than hopping (Item #58) and galloping (Item #64). It requires the combination of a step and a hop into a regular and rhythmic pattern.

TASK DESCRIPTION:

The child is able to combine steps and hops into skipping movements for five or six yards.

SAMPLE OBJECTIVE:

To refine gross motor skills.

SUGGESTED ACTIVITIES:

1. Have children practice moving around the room taking short steps and large steps.
2. Have children practice jumping around using both legs. Follow this activity with hops on one leg and then the other.
3. Ask the children to combine the movements into a step and a hop. Slowly clap out a rhythm of "step and hop" for children to follow as they practice. Increase the speed of movement as the children achieve proficiency.
4. Use the story *Little Red Riding Hood*. The children can practice skipping like Little Red Riding Hood in a dramatization of the story. (The wolf mask from Item #9 can be reused in this activity).

 **catches ball (II)**

Catches 3" to 4" thrown ball using both hands.

DEVELOPMENTAL SIGNIFICANCE:

This item is an advanced version of Item #59. In this item, the size of the ball is reduced. There is also an expectation that the child will catch the ball with the hands, rather than using hands, arms and body together.

TASK DESCRIPTION:

Child is able to catch a ball 3" to 4" in diameter just using the hands when it is thrown from a distance of at least four feet.

SAMPLE OBJECTIVE:

To develop gross motor skills.
To develop fine motor skills.

SUGGESTED ACTIVITIES:

1. The same activities suggested for Item #59 are appropriate for this item, but use smaller balls. Begin with a ball about 8" in diameter and follow with progressively smaller balls.
2. Play "catch" with the child using a ball about 8" in diameter. At first, let the child use the arms in addition to the hands for assistance. Eventually, encourage the use of the hands only.
3. Make sure that children stand close to each other during the first catching games and then step back as they become more proficient. The ball should be thrown underhanded to the child catching.

 **walks backwards**

Can walk backwards in a defined space without bumping others.

DEVELOPMENTAL SIGNIFICANCE:

The child's gross motor skills and balance are being evaluated in this item. The child must "trust" her body movements in order to feel comfortable performing this task. This item reflects the child's increasing motor functioning as well as trust in her body.

TASK DESCRIPTION:

Child is able to walk backwards in a defined space without bumping others. Specifically, designate an area (between two barriers or in a small room, for example) and have the child walk backwards through that area without bumping into anything or anyone.

SAMPLE OBJECTIVE:

To develop gross motor skills.

SUGGESTED ACTIVITIES:

1. Play a game in which the child walks sideways, first being led by another child, and then alone.
2. Have two children hold hands while standing face to face. To music, have one child walk forward and the other backward. Stop the music and change directions.
3. Encourage the child to take backward as well as forward steps when dancing.
4. Make the Magic Movie Camera shown on the next page. Fill the camera with activity cards with instructions such as "Walk Backwards" and representative illustrations. One by one, pull the cards out and have the children perform the activity shown on each card. Pretend to film the children's movements.

Magic Movie Camera

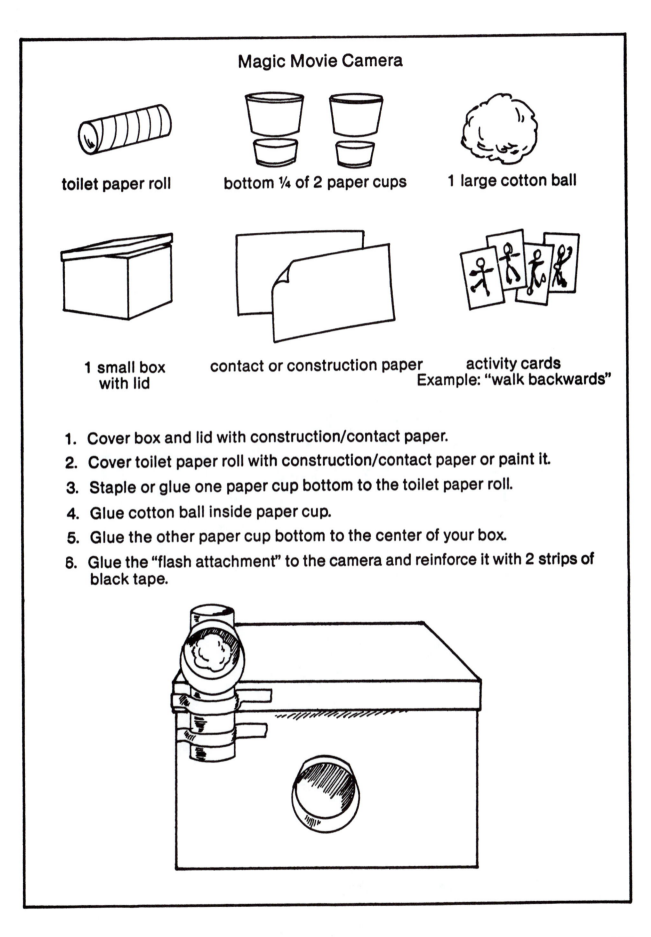

toilet paper roll

bottom ¼ of 2 paper cups

1 large cotton ball

1 small box with lid

contact or construction paper

activity cards
Example: "walk backwards"

1. Cover box and lid with construction/contact paper.
2. Cover toilet paper roll with construction/contact paper or paint it.
3. Staple or glue one paper cup bottom to the toilet paper roll.
4. Glue cotton ball inside paper cup.
5. Glue the other paper cup bottom to the center of your box.
6. Glue the "flash attachment" to the camera and reinforce it with 2 strips of black tape.

Chapter 7

Humanics National Child Assessment Form: Hygiene and Self-Help Development

ITEMS 73-90

 **allows sufficient time for toilet needs**

Alerts teacher of needs.
Controls need until toilet is used.

DEVELOPMENTAL SIGNIFICANCE:

This item reflects the child's awareness of specific body functions. After the child becomes cognizant of her bathroom needs, she must alert the teacher of the need and exercise control until the bathroom facilities are used.

TASK DESCRIPTION:

The child alerts the teacher of toilet needs and controls them until she can go to the bathroom.

SAMPLE OBJECTIVE:

To promote hygiene and self-help needs with reference to toilet needs.

SUGGESTED ACTIVITIES:

1. Plan a lesson on *Bathroom Manners*. Talk about ways of asking to go to the bathroom. Remind the children of proper ways of using the toilet, using paper and washing hands.
2. Allow children to go to the toilet before engaging in outside activities, taking trips, or playing away from bathroom facilities.
3. Make sure that bathroom doors open easily and do not "lock" the children in. Entry and departure from toilets should be so easy that the children feel secure at all times. Lights should be left on.
4. Have a bathroom badge or cardboard key which is worn or carried by the child needing to use the bathroom. As an alternative, make a "Stop/Go" bathroom sign to hang on the bathroom door to indicate when the bathroom is or is not occupied. (See illustration on next page). Check toilet facilities after use and commend children for correct manners.

STOP

1. Cut out circles.
2. Color "Stop" red.
3. Color "Go" green.
4. Glue together.
5. Make a yarn loop to go over door handle.
6. Put on restroom door.

GO

GO

dresses self (I)

Puts on basic clothing such as shirts, pants, and socks without adult supervision.

DEVELOPMENTAL SIGNIFICANCE:

This item deals with children taking responsibility for putting their own clothes on. It indicates increasing independence from adults in performing a basic daily task. It also indicates early proficiency in motor development, as buttons, snaps, and zippers have to be manipulated. Dressing herself will add to the child's understanding of body design, symmetry, and logical sequences and patterns of dressing.

TASK DESCRIPTION:

The child is able to put on shirts, pants, and socks without adult supervision.

SAMPLE OBJECTIVE:

To promote self-help skills in the area of dress.

SUGGESTED ACTIVITIES:

1. Play the *Sock It To Me Game.* Collect a pile of multi-colored outsized socks. Mix them up, and have the children sort them into pairs and pull them on.
2. Play the *Hobo Dressing Game.* Have a box of outsized clothes ready. Make a set of picture cards (if desired, use the illustrations on the next page) to match the items in the box. Show the group a picture card (for example, of a blue shirt) and have one of the children find the matching item and put it on.
3. Encourage doll play which includes changing doll clothes.
4. Make the dress up box a regular feature of informal play.

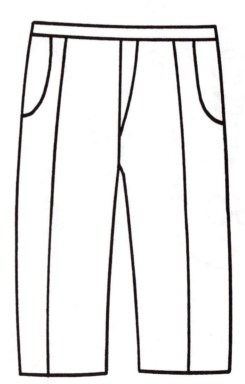

knows identifying information

Says own first and last name, age, and sex.

DEVELOPMENTAL SIGNIFICANCE:

The ability of a young child to recognize identifying personal information reveals continuing development of a sense of self. Her name is unique and distinguishes her from others. Knowing her sex and age are further elements which contribute to her individuality. Her ability to express this identifying information helps to build her confidence, strengthens self esteem and supports independence.

TASK DESCRIPTION:

The child is able to say her first and last name, sex, and age when asked to do so.

SAMPLE OBJECTIVE:

To promote those characteristics of self-help dealing with identifying information.

SUGGESTED ACTIVITIES:

1. Ask the children to draw pictures of themselves for a bulletin board. Write their first and last names, sex, and ages on the individual pictures.
2. Use a puppet to play the *Introduction Game*. The teacher "talks" through a puppet and each child responds.
   > Teacher: Hello! My name is Paul Puppet. I am a boy. I am four years old.
   > Child: I'm pleased to meet you. My name is _ _ _ _ _ . I am a _ _ _ _ _ _. I am _ _ _ years old.
   > (Continue around the group)
3. Make an Indian Girl picture graph which shows the full name, sex, and age of each child. (See illustration.)

Happy Birthday

Enlarge to life size.

Happy Birthday Indian Girl.

uses spoon and fork

Eats with spoon or fork according to the type of food served.

DEVELOPMENTAL SIGNIFICANCE:

The ability to eat with a fork or spoon indicates two elements of continuing growth and maturity. It shows skill in manipulating utensils in a particular social setting. It also requires differentiation between soft and hard foods to determine which utensil to use.

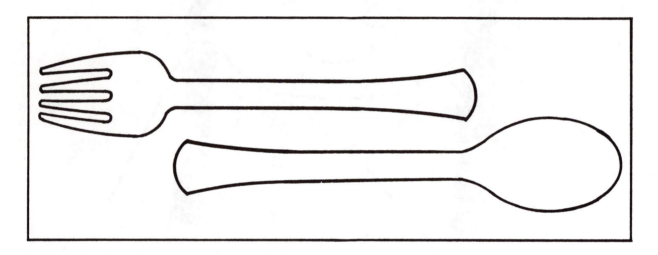

TASK DESCRIPTION:

The child uses a fork to eat firmly textured foods such as bite-sized pieces of meat and vegetables, and a spoon for such items as apple sauce, soup, or pudding.

SAMPLE OBJECTIVE:

To promote self-help skills in eating.

SUGGESTED ACTIVITIES:

1. Turn snack time into the LUNCH BUNCH BRUNCH. Set up a restaurant table and explain what hostesses, waiters, and "bus boys" do. Talk about the proper way to use eating utensils at a restaurant. Allow the children to take on the roles of restaurant helpers in the serving of snacks. Give stamps, stars, or stickers as awards to the best helpers. Give similar awards to the children with best table manners. (SUPER SPOON and FANTASTIC FORK CERTIFICATES might be useful).
2. Use the pattern on next page to make each child a placemat. Print each child's name on her placemat and let the children color their placemats as they please. Laminate the placemats and let the children use them all year long at snack time.

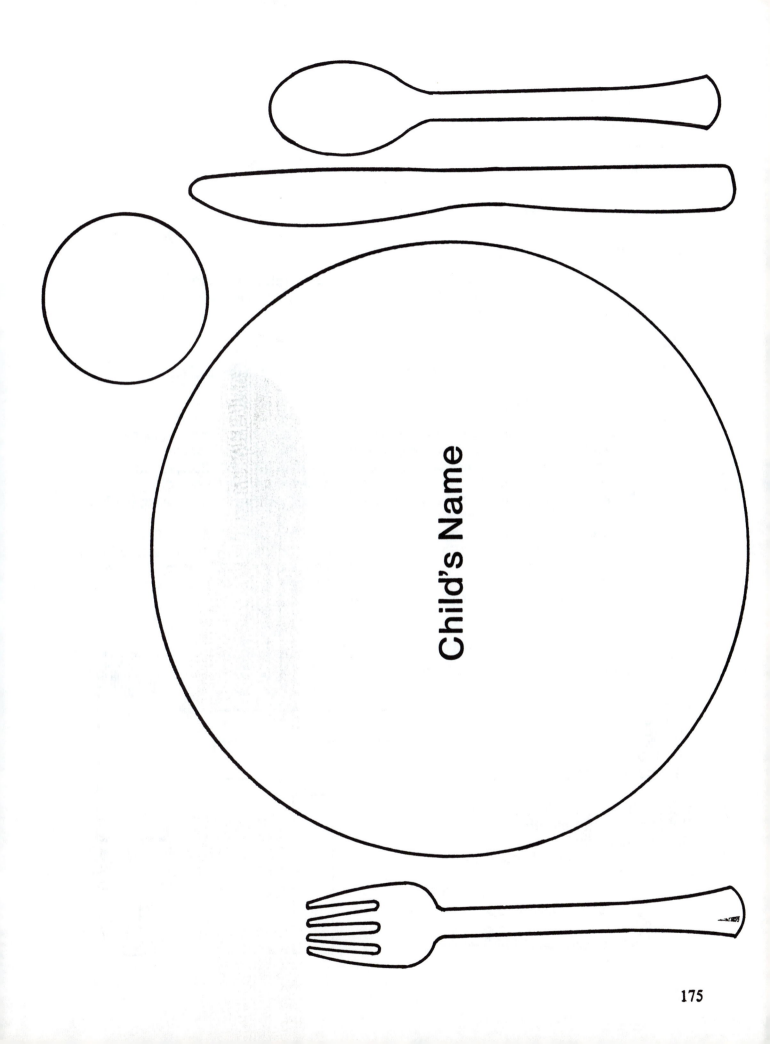

Child's Name

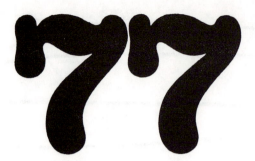

puts things away

Follows directions in putting things away.

DEVELOPMENTAL SIGNIFICANCE:

The child is beginning to accept new responsibilities for order and cleanliness in the classroom. He has a part to play in maintaining a satisfactory system of organization in the room. Skill in following directions is reinforced.

TASK DESCRIPTION:

The child places objects in their proper storage areas at the request of the teacher.

SUGGESTED ACTIVITIES:

1. Place labels and picture cards on each designated storage area. For example, a picture of a block and the word "block" might be placed on the block shelf or box.
2. Draw outlines of some objects next to hooks, on shelves, or on the floor, to show where such items as carpentry tools, trucks or special equipment are to be stored.
3. Identify special helpers to be in charge of collecting puzzle pieces, cleaning brushes, cleaning shelves or folding clothes.
4. Select a special center in the room and have the children look at it closely. Using a *Terrible Troll Puppet*, play the *Terrible Troll's Tantalizing Toy Game*. Ask all the children to close their eyes while the Terrible Troll steals a tantalizing toy. The group has to guess which toy is missing and remember how it should be replaced. Let the children take turns at being the Terrible Troll.

Terrible Troll Puppet

You will need:

Glue
Tube sock
Plastic eyes
Scrap of colorful felt
(orange or purple)

Cut 2 felt pieces to form a T (eyebrows and nose).
Cut felt piece for mouth.
Glue parts to sock.
Add hair (green yarn) if you wish.

Mouth

length of hair

cleans spills

Cleans up spills with direction from teacher.

DEVELOPMENTAL SIGNIFICANCE:

This item is designed to indicate that individual children can accept social responsibility for mishaps or accidents, whether they are directly accountable or not. Cleaning up a spill requires good social sense and shows attention to hygiene and self-help tasks.

TASK DESCRIPTION:

The child is able to clean up liquid spills from table tops or floors with a sponge or towel.

SAMPLE OBJECTIVE:

To promote self-help skills and social awareness.

SUGGESTED ACTIVITIES:

1. Have a *Squeeze and Squirt Time* where the teacher squeezes some water from a liquid detergent container into a sink, or onto a protected table top, and demonstrates how to wipe it up. The children take turns squeezing the container and cleaning up the water.
2. Use a sponge and water basin to give children practice in squeezing water out of a sponge.
3. On paper, fingerpaint a large "S" for "Super Spill" for each child. Let them dry and pin one to each child's shirt.

79

plays actively

**Plays actively on the playground
without the teacher's constant supervision.**

DEVELOPMENTAL SIGNIFICANCE:

This item suggests that the child is able to manage her time on the playground in her own way. It indicates that the child feels good enough about herself not to need constant adult supervision and that she can take responsibility for her activities in a safe manner.

TASK DESCRIPTION:

While on the playground, the child is actively involved in playful situations without the teacher's constant supervision.

SAMPLE OBJECTIVE:

To promote self-help skills.

SUGGESTED ACTIVITIES:

1. Discuss appropriate outdoor behavior. Running, jumping, loud talking, etc., are some things that can best be done outdoors rather than indoors. Include a discussion of the equipment in your playground and how to use it safely.
2. Offer group activities outdoors, particularly for children who are not comfortable playing alone. Gradually encourage each child to plan her own time a good portion of outdoor playtime.
3. Enforce safe play outdoors. Unnecessary roughness must be eliminated for the safety of all. The children should participate in making the rules for appropriate outdoor behavior. They can also participate in deciding the consequences of breaking the rules.

**80** manages bathroom facilities

Manages bathroom facilities according to conventional routines.

DEVELOPMENTAL SIGNIFICANCE:

This item is an extension of Item #73. It requires more sophisticated facility on the child's part since she must be able to carry out toilet needs rather than merely alerting the teacher. It is, therefore, a more advanced indication of the child's ability to rely on herself to take care of personal needs.

TASK DESCRIPTION:

The child is able to go to the bathroom, prepare herself, and use the facility appropriately. She must be able to follow normal practices of hygiene and replace her clothing. All this must be done without assistance.

SAMPLE OBJECTIVE:

To encourage hygiene skills.

SUGGESTED ACTIVITIES:

1. Have the child practice dressing and undressing a doll. The child can also practice taking the doll to the toilet and going through the entire toilet routine.
2. Be sure the children are given ample opportunity to use the bathroom. Use the chart of bathroom behaviors which follows.

Mr. Owl

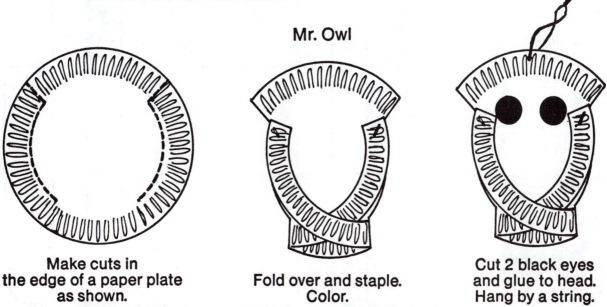

Make cuts in the edge of a paper plate as shown.

Fold over and staple. Color.

Cut 2 black eyes and glue to head. Hang by a string.

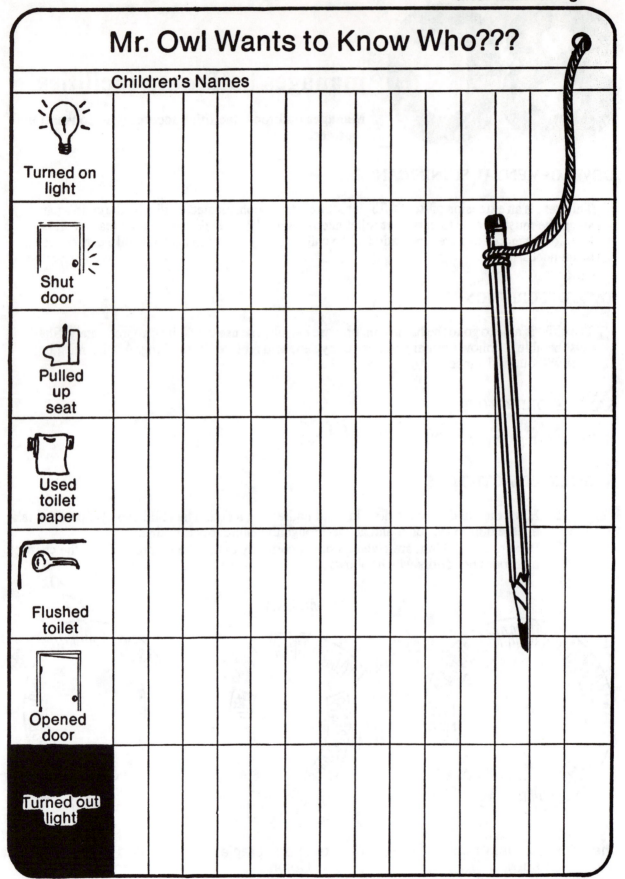

Tie grease pencil here after laminating

Mr. Owl Wants to Know Who???

Children's Names

Turned on light									
Shut door									
Pulled up seat									
Used toilet paper									
Flushed toilet									
Opened door									
Turned out light									

dresses self (II)

Is able to manipulate buttons, zippers and other fasteners, and to tie shoes.

DEVELOPMENTAL SIGNIFICANCE:

This item is an extension of Item #74. A child's mastery of this self-help skill indicates her increasing sense of independence, as well as maturation in fine motor skill development. She will feel self-pride and a sense of accomplishment in independently choosing and putting on all her clothes. Her ability to master dressing shows responsibility for managing an important routine that is necessary for home and school.

TASK DESCRIPTION:

The child is able to completely dress herself, including independently manipulating all types of closures and fasteners, and tying shoes.

SAMPLE OBJECTIVE:

To promote self-help skills.

SUGGESTED ACTIVITIES:

1. Read aloud books about dressing, clothes, proper attire. Some books that young children would enjoy hearing are:
   What Should a Hippo Wear? — Jane Sutton
   How Do I Put It On? — Shigeo Watanabe
   I Can Dress Myself — Dick Brunna
2. Practice buttoning, zipping and tying on commercially purchased materials such as *Dapper Dan* or *Dressy Bessie*. Also, real baby clothes that can be used for Teddy Bear or large doll dress-up give children excellent hands-on experience in buttoning, snapping, and zipping.
3. Play "TAKE A ZIP AND PASS IT ON." Divide a small group into two teams and line up each team. Take two zippered coats with zippers of similar difficulty and give one coat to the first child in each line to put on independently. On the signal "go" from the teacher, the first child in each team has the second team member zip up her coat. Then, the coat wearer must unzip the coat, take it off, give it to the second team member (who did the zipping). The game continues in the same manner until all children have zipped and unzipped the coat. A variation of this game, where there are very few children in the group, is to have just one team.
4. TIE A BUTTERFLY — Use this technique to show small children how to tie their shoes. After crossing the shoe laces, make two loops (butterfly wings) with the laces. Next, tuck one "wing" under and through. To help young children manipulate the ties, as well as secure the middle of the bow, use a substitute "finger" such as a spring clothespin or long bobby pin or hair clip. Before pulling the shoe lace tightly, the "finger" should be removed. If desired, have the children cut out paper shoes to practice tying, using the pattern on the following page.

181

Tie a Butterfly with your own shoe.

1. Have each child cut out shoe.
2. Use hole punchers on black dots.
3. Have each child lace shoe.

Suggestion: Reinforce shoes with poster paper.

helps prepare for activity

Helps set out project materials on table.

DEVELOPMENTAL SIGNIFICANCE:

The receptiveness of a child to help prepare for various center activities indicates that she is becoming responsible for herself in socially acceptable ways. The child who can contribute to the preparation of a particular activity is beginning to recognize the connection between getting materials organized and carrying out a successful activity. Mastery of this item implies that the child is acquiring a sense of order. She is aware that certain things within her life (i.e., paints, paper, blocks, housekeeping equipment, and so on) have a particular place and function.

TASK DESCRIPTION:

With appropriate teacher direction, the child is able to gather the items needed for an activity and set them out in an orderly manner at the assigned center.

SAMPLE OBJECTIVE:

To promote self-help skills.

SUGGESTED ACTIVITIES:

1. Read books about classroom help and developing a spirit of sharing work as well as fun, such as:
   > *Doing Things Together* — Coral Barkin and Elizabeth James
   > *My Nursery School* — Harlow Rockwell (ages 3-5)
   > *Bubba and Babba* — Maria Polushkin
2. Make materials easily accessible to children. Place all supplies that are needed for daily classroom activities on low shelves and organize materials according to use. For example, store all paper materials, pasting supplies, painting mediums, etc. together. It is desirable to keep a limited number of supplies out and then replenish and rotate the materials as activities and needs change.
3. Help children be organized when gathering materials for center activities by providing a carrying device. A cafeteria tray, plastic dishwashing pan or bucket all make excellent carryalls for cumbersome supplies. Paper plates or styrofoam meat trays can be used for individual activities.
4. Assign center helpers on a rotational basis so each child will have experience in preparation of various centers and activities. The same children who are assigned "set-up duty" could also have "clean-up" responsibility.
5. Make a "Happy Helper" for each child, complete with name. (See pattern on the next page.) Let the children color the Happy Helpers and cut them out. Laminate them. Staple two green pieces of paper 12" by 9" together to form a secret pocket in which to store all the Happy Helpers. Each day, pull out enough Happy Helpers as children are needed for assigned tasks. Tape each day's Happy Helpers to a cupboard door or other appropriate place so children will know who are that day's happy helpers.
6. Read or show a filmstrip of the story "The Elves and the Shoemaker."

Happy Helper

83 cares for toys

Takes care of toys and materials.

DEVELOPMENTAL SIGNIFICANCE:

The ability of a child to care for her toys and materials indicates that she is developing a sense of responsibility for herself as well as to the group. She is accepting the obligation of taking care for the materials and toys that she uses and is beginning to realize that playing creates an obligation to put away and clean up. By successfully meeting this responsibility, she demonstrates her continuing desire to become self-reliant as well as to meet a social responsibility to her play group.

TASK DESCRIPTION:

The child is observed 1) using toys in a creative but appropriate manner (i.e., dolls or puppets are friendly but do not hit or fight); 2) returning toys and materials to their proper storage places; and 3) telling adults about broken or missing parts from toys or materials.

SAMPLE OBJECTIVE:

To promote self-help skills.

SUGGESTED ACTIVITIES:

1. Read a book about caring for toys, such as:
   William's Doll — Charlotte Shapiro Zoloton
   Izzie — Susan Pearson
   Natasha's New Bull — Frank Francis
2. Use an old torn and tattered doll or torn-up, rusted truck as a motivational device for a group language experience story. Allow the children to take turns dictating sentences to the teacher who will write the story on a large chart or blackboard. As a story-starter title, use, "The Trials and Tribulations of Torn and Tattered Toys."
3. Bring in several antique toys or visit a toy museum. Try to impress upon children that these were toys with which children actually played many years ago. The toys were so loved, though, that they were not mistreated and that's why they are old but still in good condition today. Have the children draw a picture of their favorite toy using the picture frame on the next page.
4. Help children in their material management by having suitable storage containers for blocks, beads, games, and so on. Once a week special helpers may be allowed to sort through certain materials so that out-of-place pieces can be replaced before they are lost or broken.

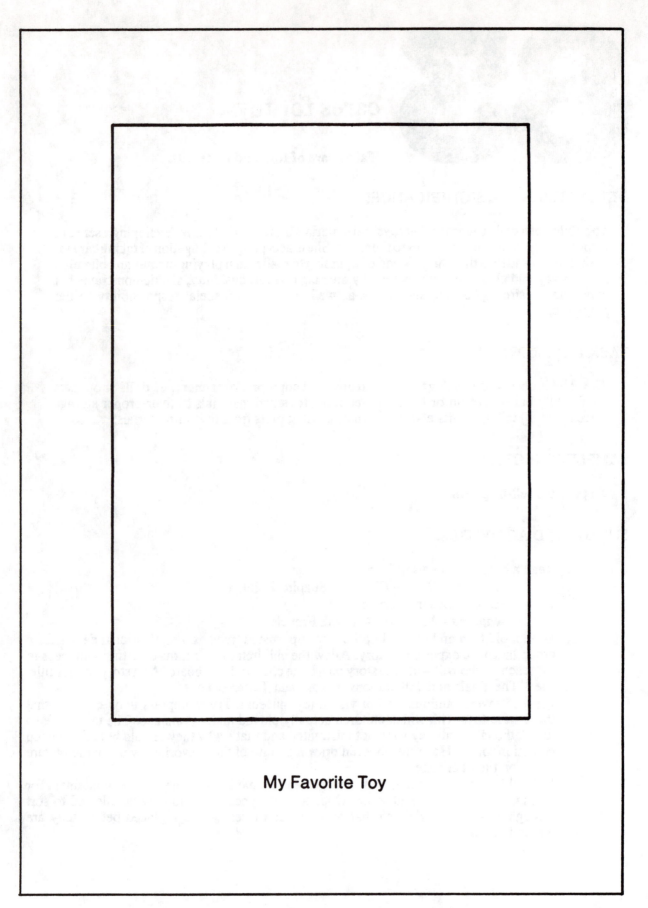

My Favorite Toy

(Paste scrap material to the mat area).

84 cares for possessions

Shows responsibility for personal possessions.

DEVELOPMENTAL SIGNIFICANCE:

This item is an extension of the previous item. Item #83, however, emphasized the child's need to care for classroom toys and materials as an individual responsibility as well as a social obligation to her class group. This item stresses the need for a child to be responsible for her own personal possessions as well. The child who independently takes care of her own personal items and materials should feel positive about herself. By showing pride in how she cares for her own belongings, she will also begin to understand the need to respect others' personal property.

TASK DESCRIPTION:

The child shows concern for her personal possessions by independently 1) placing her personal dressing items in the correct areas (i.e., coat on a hanger, gloves in cubby, paint shirt on a hook); 2) storing her personal nonclothing items in proper storage places (i,.e., lunch box on the table, book bag in the closet, work papers or projects in individual's cubby); 3) coming to school and leaving school grounds with her personal possessions intact.

SAMPLE OBJECTIVE:

To promote self-help skills.

SUGGESTED ACTIVITIES:

1. Read the book, *Molly's Moe* by Kay Choraco. This delightful story will tie in well with the theme of being responsible for one's possessions.
2. Assign a "cubby" or shoe box for each child to have as her personal storage area. Write each child's name on the assigned area and impress upon the children that each child must respect the others' personal possessions. Also, assign special places for each child to hang her coat, put her lunch box, place her book bag, and so on.
3. Suggest to parents that children carry book bags or totes. Such a book bag usually insures that work papers, projects and special notices make it home, rather than getting lost on the way to the car or bus. A simple burlap tote bag could be constructed by room mothers or aides and decorated by each child as an art project.
4. Set up a "SHOW AND TELL" schedule for the class. Instead of having one day with

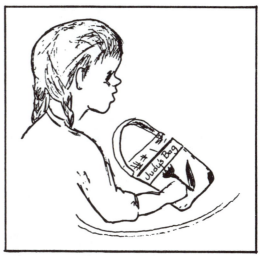

twenty-plus show and tellers, divide the group into small sections and spread out "Show and Tell" for five days, having four or five children share per day. The children can be designated as Monday, Tuesday, Wednesday, Thursday, Friday. Notices can go home to inform parents of their child's "day." Certain SHOW AND TELL weeks could have special themes. For example, during National Book week, ask the children to bring in their favorite book, or after Christmas, allow the children to share their favorite game or toy with their classmates.

5. Help children to be responsible for their own things by refusing to hold their money, coats, jewelry and so on. Encourage them to be organized with their possessions by providing each of them with an envelope or plastic bag to hold loose items.

6. As a combination art and writing lesson, have children design their own clothes "labels." Give each child a small strip of white cloth about 1" x 3". Let the children print their names — first and a last initial — on the tag using a permanent marker. (Help with the printing if necessary). If desired, have the children decorate the tags with permanent markers. Use masking tape to hold down the material so it will not wrinkle while the children write on and decorate it. Make several tags and give them to mother as a "gift" to sew into school clothes.

tries new food

Samples a "taste-test" of new food when it is served.

DEVELOPMENTAL SIGNIFICANCE:

Trying a new food indicates that the child is willing to experiment with different flavors and textures and is open to new experiences. The mastery of this item implies that the child is able to adapt to social situations which may include unfamiliar dishes served in uncustomary ways. By accepting new food experiences, children can make a transference association when attempting unusual and previously untried situations in other areas.

TASK DESCRIPTION:

The child will try a sample "taste-test" of unfamiliar food when it is served to her.

SAMPLE OBJECTIVE:

To encourage self-help skills and to promote proper nutrition.

SUGGESTED ACTIVITIES:

1. Read books about food. Some such books are:
   The Hungry Leprechaun — Mary Calhoun
   The Very Hungry Caterpillar — Eric Carle
   Little Bear's Pancake Party — Janice Brustlein
   Green Eggs and Ham — Theodor Seuss Geisel
   Scrambled Eggs Super — Theodor Seuss Geisel
   The Steam Shovel that Wouldn't Eat Dirt — Walker Retan
   Munch — Alexandra Wallner
   Don't Forget the Bacon! — Pat Hutchins
2. Give out "TERRIFIC TASTE TESTER" awards (or badges or stickers) to children who try one bite of each new food that they are served.
3. Have special international cooking days. Invite parents who can cook specialty foods in the classroom. A Chinese parent may volunteer to make egg rolls, a British parent, kidney pie, and so on. American parents may also wish to fix recipes that have been in their family for generations. Children and adults may also enjoy an International Foods Festival with all parents contributing food. For international cooking days, have the class make chef's hats and menus as shown on the next page.
4. Children can become "involved" in new foods by participating in the shopping, cooking and serving of the food. Let them wear their chef hats from Activity #3.
5. Make a language experience chart. Write descriptive words such as *musty, sliced, juicy, meaty, gritty, crunchy,* and so on. Paste either magazine pictures of food or actual labels from boxes or cans of food under each title.
6. Let each child "tell" her favorite recipe for a food she has tried and would recommend to her friends. As she "tells" you how to fix it, write down her instructions on a piece of paper. Let her draw the illustration. Bind all the class recipes into a HIGHLY RECOMMENDED CLASS COOKBOOK!

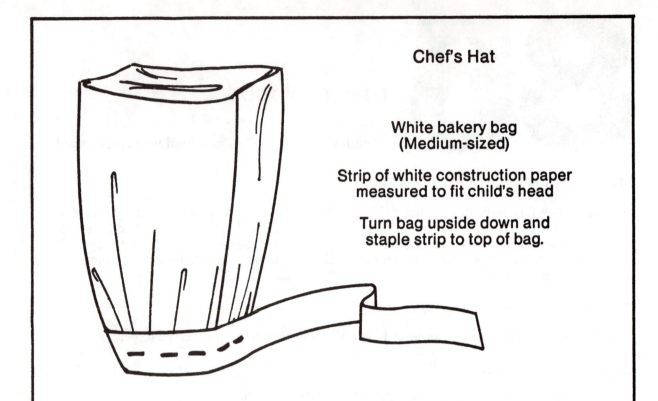

Chef's Hat

White bakery bag
(Medium-sized)

Strip of white construction paper
measured to fit child's head

Turn bag upside down and
staple strip to top of bag.

Menu

Glue white paper to colored
paper 9" x 12"

Fold in half so that the
white paper is inside.

Write the word "Menu" on
the front and decorate.

List your international
foods and the parents
who helped inside.

identifies food

Classifies food belonging to the four basic food groups.

DEVELOPMENTAL SIGNIFICANCE:

Item #86 indicates the importance of a child's being aware of the relationship between selecting a variety of foods and having good eating habits. By learning that foods can be classified into four basic groups and that meals should consist of foods from each group, she will be able to understand the nutritional significance of eating foods from all groups.

TASK DESCRIPTION:

The child will be able to classify foods into the basic food group categories — 1) Meat, 2) Vegetables and Fruit, 3) Cereals and Grains and 4) Milk and Dairy Products. The child will classify the foods by 1) naming foods that belong to each group; 2) sorting foods (pictures, labels, etc.) into proper food groups; and 3) planning a meal which includes food from each group (optional).

SAMPLE OBJECTIVE:

To encourage hygiene skills through nutrition awareness.

SUGGESTED ACTIVITIES:

1. Introduce one basic food group per day. For example, Monday could be meat day; Tuesday, fruit and vegetables; Wednesday, cereals and grains; and Thursday, milk and dairy products. Friday might be a culminating day where activities are combined and ideas are pulled together so children can understand the importance of combining food groups. Some suggested activities to use for each special day are:
   a. Read books about the food group.
   b. Cut out pictures or draw favorite foods from that group.
   c. Ask a community resource person such as the milkman, produce man, butcher or baker, to come in and talk about a food group.
   d. Go on a field trip to visit a dairy or meat-packing company, produce market, bakery, etc.
   e. Cook simple foods or snacks that contain foods from the group that is being studied.
   f. Incorporate arts and crafts ideas around each basic group, such as cutting fresh fruits and vegetables into shapes and putting the shapes together to form edible characters, such as CARROT CHARACTER or FRUIT FUN FELLOWS.
   g. Have the children complete the worksheet that follows, "What Shall We Have for Dinner?" to reinforce what they've learned.
2. Guess What We Are Having For Dinner?
   Take a number of paper plates, divide each plate into four sections so that one food for

each food group can be represented, and give each child one plate. Let the children draw or cut pictures for each food to be represented and arrange the foods on their plates. As an extension, play this game with small groups. Each child can chose (or the teacher can select) a dinner "guest" to come for dinner. The "guest" must name the foods on the plate she is served, and then the groups of each food. Then switch, so that the guest is now the "host" and her "guest" must do the same before she "eats" her dinner.

3. As a language experience activity, have each child recite her favorite dinner menu. Make sure that she names one food from each basic food group. Write down her menu. Attach the menu to her "plate" from Activity #2 and display them on a bulletin board labeled, for example, COOKS' CORNER or FAVORITE FOODS.

What Shall We Have for Dinner?

1. Circle 1 meat with orange crayon.
2. Circle 1 fruit with red crayon.
3. Circle 1 vegetable with blue crayon.
4. Circle 1 bread with green crayon.

fish

carrots

bread

peas

rolls

cherries

pineapple

chicken

apple

demonstrates judgment

Exhibits proper judgment and understands safety principles.

DEVELOPMENTAL SIGNIFICANCE:

A child exhibits increasing maturity when she demonstrates behavior that is appropriate to particular situations. The child who displays correct judgment in various circumstances is incorporating her previously-learned experiences and applying this learning to present situations. In using this judgment she is choosing to exhibit appropriate or inappropriate behavior. The result of her choice in behavior will help her learn to accept the responsibility for her actions. It is important that the child be aware that improper behavior which is also unsafe may result in serious consequences to herself and to others.

TASK DESCRIPTION:

The child demonstrates her knowledge of basic safety principles by exhibiting appropriate behavior for the activity in which she is engaged.

SAMPLE OBJECTIVE:

To promote self-help skills.

SUGGESTED ACTIVITIES:

1. Read books that deal with decision making and acting in appropriate ways. Suggestions are:
   Try It Again Sam — Judith Viorst
   Safety Can Be Fun — Munro Leaf
   No! No! — Lois Myller
   Rufus the Doofus — Ned Delaney
   Swimming — Leo Lionni
   Noisy Nancy Norris — LouAnn Bigge Gaeddert
2. Discuss the meaning of appropriate behavior. Tell children that the importance of the way in which they behave is usually not whether it is bad or good, but rather whether it is RIGHT FOR THE ACTIVITY. For example, whistling or making noise is not bad behavior, but it is inappropriate during story time. Whistling would be appropriate behavior, however, during a music activity song that asks the child to participate.
3. As a follow-up to Activity #2, make an APPROPRIATE BEHAVIOR CHART. On the chart, label columns Classroom, Hall, Play Yard, Lunchroom, Bus Area, etc. Have children take turns selecting picture cards (or word cards) that have various people (or children) exhibiting different behaviors. Discuss which place the activity might be appropriate. Attach the card in the correct column. Continue until you have discussed and placed all cards.
4. Reward children in the class who have used appropriate behavior (perhaps when most of

the others did not). Use a certificate that says: I (child's name) showed Ap"PRO"priate behavior today (date) by (describe behavior).

5. Discuss classroom safety, as well as safety on the playground, hall, lunchroom, bus area, etc. Play "SAFETY SLEUTHING." Divide children into small groups of Safety Detectives. (Provide the children with make-believe magnifying glasses and "Sherlock Holmes" hats if desired). Designate areas that need to be checked out for safety hazards or potentially dangerous items. As each team finds "clues," (i.e., safety hazards) have them tell their teacher/aide, who lists all the danger areas. After all areas have been surveyed, let each child tell or "read" about her finds. Compile a list labeled "CLUES AND DO'S FOR SAFETY"(examples: watch out for loose bricks in the walk, stay away from the electrical outlets, etc.) and post the list.

6. Invite community resource people (e.g., fireman, police, coast guard, etc.) to discuss safety in the home and neighborhood. Most communities have services that will provide school presentations.

recognizes weather

Understand weather concepts, identifies play activities suitable for weather conditions, and dresses appropriately for the weather.

DEVELOPMENTAL SIGNIFICANCE:

This item emphasizes the need of the child to become aware of her environment through understanding some basic weather concepts. It is important that, in addition to knowing about different kinds of weather, she be flexible in adapting to weather changes.

TASK DESCRIPTION:

The child should understand weather concepts by being able to tell the difference between basic weather conditions — hot, warm, cold temperatures; wet or dry; cloudy (overcast) or sunny; windy or calm; and rain, snow, or hail. The child should name play activities that would be suitable for varying weather conditions and identify appropriate clothes for the play activities.

SAMPLE OBJECTIVE:

To promote self-help skills.

SUGGESTED ACTIVITIES:

1. Read books that deal with weather concepts. Some suggestions are:
   The Storm Book — Charollotte Shapiro
   Harrison Loved His Umbrella — Rhoda Levine
   Beware the Polar! Bear! Safety on Ice — Miriam Burt Young
   The Sun, the Wind, the Sea and the Rain — Miriam Schlein
2. Appoint a WEATHERMAN/PERSON as a regular helper duty. Have him/her report on the daily forecast during the morning circle activity time. Some type of weather chart which has a moveable pointer would be helpful.
3. WARDROBE FOR WORRIED WEATHER WATCHERS.
   Bring in a variety of children's clothes and weather accessories — umbrellas, boots, scarves, etc. Place these in a box or lay them out on a low table. Make up stories about different types of weather. Ask for volunteers to come up and select appropriate attire for the weather condition you have described. A large doll or animal who could be dressed up in the clothes might be a fun touch. As an alternative, use the paper doll from Item #42 and the clothes patterns shown on the next pages.
4. Each week, make a simple wall chart (or individual ditto for older children) labeled WEEKDAY WEATHER (WHETHER WE LIKE IT OR NOT), which lists the days of the week. Each day, have the children draw in the appropriate weather symbol under that day's heading to reflect what the weather is doing.
5. Make WANDA WEATHER GIRL or WILLIAM WEATHER GUY puppets.
   Cut a basic unisex doll shape out of oak tag or poster board for each child. Prepare a set of weather conditions (e.g., "Rain") and play activity (e.g., "Playing on the beach") cards, and have each child draw one. The child will design appropriate clothes for her puppet with material and paper scraps. Display the puppets on a bulletin board with the

caption WEATHER WATCHERS' WARDROBE.

6. A language experience activity could also be used as a follow-up to Activity #5. Children could write: "My puppet's name is _____. He/she is wearing _____ because (the weather or activity) _____."
Attach this writing to the board where the puppet is displayed.

long sleeve shirt

sandals

short sleeve shirt

long pants

shorts

sneakers

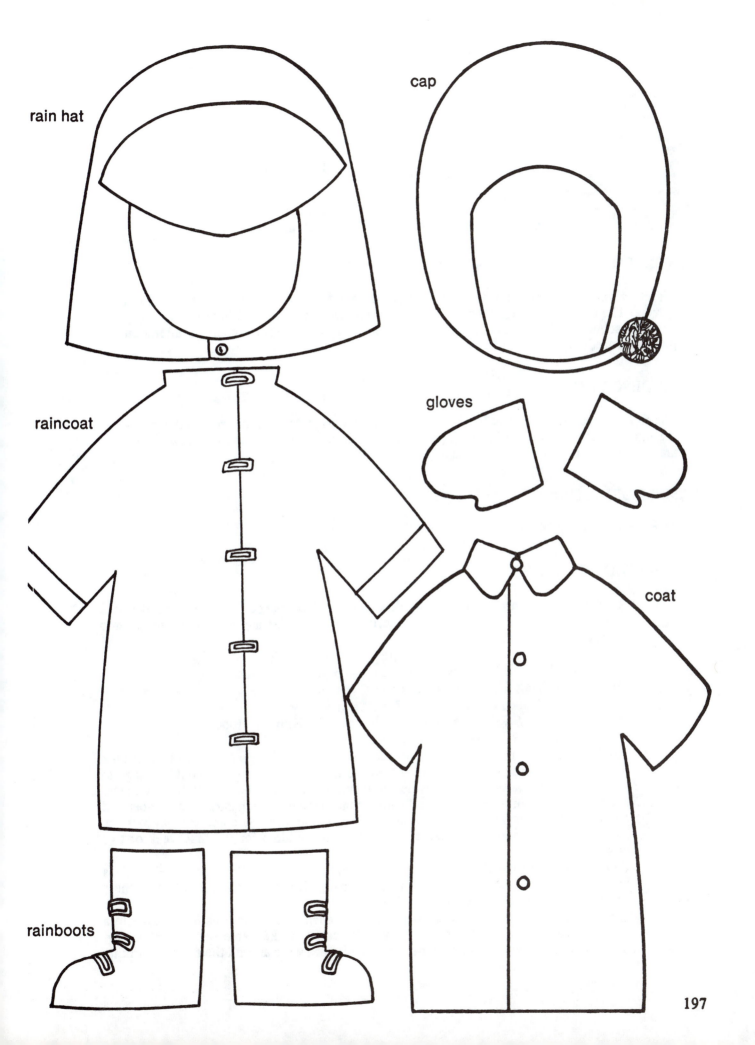

rain hat

cap

raincoat

gloves

coat

rainboots

197

understands travel

**Locates classroom in the morning;
knows after school pick-up procedure.**

DEVELOPMENTAL SIGNIFICANCE:

The child is more independent when she understands the travel patterns in coming to school and leaving. The child shows self-confidence and self-reliance when she is able to find her way about the school and into her classroom in the morning, and when she remembers the afternoon pick-up procedure.

TASK DESCRIPTION:

The child independently locates her classroom (or other designated waiting area) in the morning and knows the after school pick-up procedure (which may include waiting in an assigned area for bus or carpool pick-up or walking with an older student).

SAMPLE OBJECTIVE:

To promote self-help skills.

SUGGESTED ACTIVITIES:

1. Read books that are written about developing independence. Two very good books which deal with the experience of exploring the unfamiliar and give some insight into problem-solving techniques are:
   Rutherford T. Find 21B — Barbra Jean Rich Rinkoff
   Little Black Bear Goes for a Walk — Bernice Freschet
2. Other books about finding new places are:
   How Do you Get There? — Hans Augusto Rey
   How Do I Go? — Mary Ann Hoberman and Norman Hoberman
   Davy Goes Places — Lois L. Lenski
3. Adults should try to organize daily procedures so the child feels comfortable about the morning and afternoon school routines. In the morning, the teacher should arrange to meet the children at the door and welcome them. The teacher should also have a master list of how each child goes home and with whom. Assigning each carpool a number and having each car display its "carpool number" will help insure fast and smooth pick-up. Pin bus numbers and child's name and address to children for the first week or two of school.
   Parents can help their children feel secure about morning and afternoon travel routines by being punctual, sending notes if a pick-up change is needed, and providing business or emergency phone numbers to the school.
4. Establish a color code in your school, assigning each teacher and his/her classroom a color. Decorate each classroom door with its color. Make name tags out of appropriately colored construction paper for the children to wear around their necks, printing

the child's name on one side and her teacher's name on the other. The first few days of school, children can use the color of their name tags to help them find the correct classroom door. As a further guide, make several "Helpful Rainbows" (see next page) to hang in school hallways to help children find their classroom and learn their teacher's name.

5. Discuss safety rules that would pertain to all modes of travel routines. List car and bus "do's," and talk about safety precautions for children who walk home (e.g., street safety, do not talk to strangers, etc.).

6. Decorate a class bulletin board with types of vehicles used in afternoon pick-up. Show school buildings, teachers, children, etc.

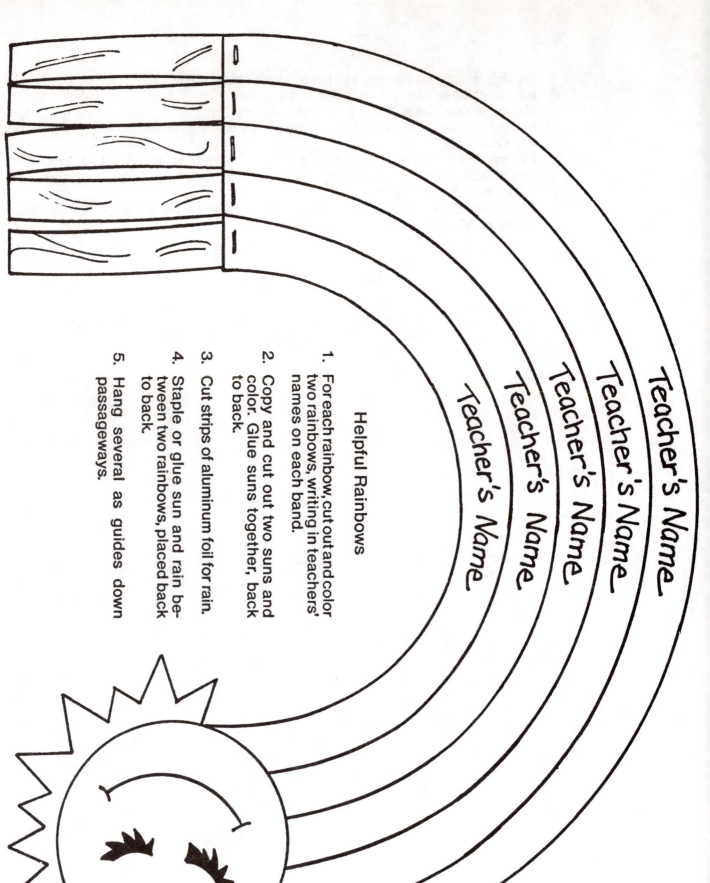

Helpful Rainbows

1. For each rainbow, cut out and color two rainbows, writing in teachers' names on each band.

2. Copy and cut out two suns and color. Glue suns together, back to back.

3. Cut strips of aluminum foil for rain.

4. Staple or glue sun and rain between two rainbows, placed back to back.

5. Hang several as guides down passageways.

Teacher's Name

Teacher's Name

Teacher's Name

Teacher's Name

Teacher's Name

Teacher's Name

90 knows address and telephone number

Knows home address or can tell where home is located; knows telephone number for home or responsible adult.

DEVELOPMENTAL SIGNIFICANCE:

The child who is able to give specific information about where she lives and recite her telephone number exhibits a developing attitude of self-sufficiency. Her ability to verbalize this important information means that the child's definition of "self" has expanded to include the location of her home and her telephone number. Her cognitive ability has expanded also. She is able to retain factual information and to respond orally upon request from adults.

TASK DESCRIPTION:

Upon request from adults, the child is able to give orally her address — house or apartment number, street name, city and state — and home phone number or number for the child's primary caretaker.

SAMPLE OBJECTIVE:

To promote self-help skills.

SUGGESTED ACTIVITIES:

1. Read books to the class which discuss the importance of knowing factual address information:

    Mike's House — Julia L. Sauer (highly recommended for children ages 5-6)
    Lost — Sonia O. Lisker
    The Telephone Telephones — Kornei Chukovsky

2. Teach a telephone unit. (Real phone kits can be borrowed from major telephone companies.) As a group activity, have children design "can" telephones by using two tin cans, 2 buttons and string. See example: ⟶

    Help children write their telephone numbers on masking tape and put the tape on both cans. Pick "talking partners." Use one telephone. Have the "caller" say to the "callee," "Is this (number on can)?" The callee will respond, "Yes, this is (number on can)." Then let the partners "switch" telephones (cans) so both partners can practice their phone numbers.

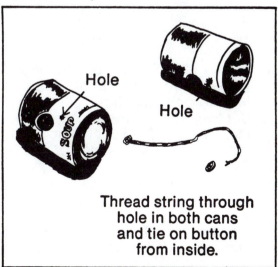

Hole

Hole

Thread string through hole in both cans and tie on button from inside.

3. Play E.T. CALL HOME! Ask a child to pretend that she is E.T. (Use a hand puppet or E.T. doll or figure). The "E.T." selected must verbally recite her home phone number. Allow each child to "phone home." As a reward, pass out badges, such as stickers that say, "I Can Call Home Like E.T.!"

4. Design an ALFIE ADDRESS ARMADILLO CENTER.
   Draw an outline of an armadillo. Print the caption "Help Alfie Cover Up!" Print child's name and address on a 3" x 5" card. Have the child practice saying her address (at home and at school). When she can say her complete address, let her color her card and paste this "armour" to Alfie Armadillo.

5. Play "Bah-Bah-Bah." In a small group situation sing "We are lost little sheep who have gone astray. Bah, bah, bah." Chose three or four "lambs" from the group. Ask each to give her address (or parts of it). After she tells her address, she choses a "new" lamb to replace her. Continue until all lost sheep are returned to the "fold."

6. Construct a HOUSE FOR A DAY center. Use a large refrigerator box or wardrobe container and decorate it as a house. Involve children in the painting, decorations, and design. When the house is finished, post the address of a child on it. This child pretends for a day that this is her house. Change the address and chose a new "resident" each day. Encourage children to read the new owner's name and address.

Mail Bag

1. Staple 2 pieces of construction paper together around three edges, leaving one edge free.
2. Cut two paper strips 4 inches wide and 14 inches long. Fold each strip in half lengthwise and glue sides together.
3. Staple strips to bag.
4. Cover staples with masking tape or decorative tape.
5. Address envelopes with students' names and addresses.
6. Play mailman. Have students identify their mail and put it in the mailbag. Have the children play several days in a row.

Chapter 8

Using The Results of The Humanics National Child Assessment Form

Once the *Humanics National Child Assessment Form* has been administered, the next task is to use the results in developing the most appropriate learning experiences for the child. An assessment tool is only as valuable as the way it is used. The results can be invaluable when considered as representations of the child's individual abilities to be used as the focus for individualized educational activities. If the results are merely set aside until the next assessment period, there is little to be gained from the assessment effort.

The Child Development Summary Profile, found on page 14 of the *H.N.C.A.F.*, is a graphic representation of the assessment results. The teacher or parent is able to see at a glance which items have stabilized as a consistent part of the child's behavioral repertoire, which have appeared but are not a regular part of her behavior, and which behaviors have not emerged. The Profile is used to begin formulating an answer to the question, "What should I teach my child?"

The *Humanics National Child Assessment Form* is useful as a screening tool to detect early signals of developmental delays or special problems. Since this is the first formal assessment observation for many children, teachers are in a unique position to determine whether a child is progressing normally in all areas of development and growth. Early detection and intervention for many potentially handicapping conditions can relieve problems that may result in irreparable harm if unnoticed.

The remainder of this chapter offers a suggested plan for incorporating the results of the *Humanics National Child Assessment Form* into an educational program for the child. First, a sample format for organizing the results of the assessment into an Individualized Educational Program is presented. Each component of an IEP is described to assist the teacher or parent in composing an educational strategy most appropriate to the needs of the particular child. The second portion of this chapter presents a complete step-by-step example of how to take the results of the *H.N.C.A.F.* and plan for particular child. The example includes a completed *H.N.C.A.F.* on one child, Angela, an IEP for her, and suggestions on how to select activities appropriate to her needs.

SCREENING FOR HANDICAPPING CONDITIONS

There is no particular formula or pattern for detecting special problems or handicapping conditions. As the observations for the *H.N.C.A.F.* are completed, however, teachers discover considerable variation from one child to the next in their developmental skills. Wide variation in skill mastery is normal in this age range. Yet, the most obvious indication that a child may have a special need is her inability to perform the basic tasks that most children of similar age have mastered.

Determining that a child has a special handicapping condition is sometimes very complicated. Although some handicapping conditions are obvious in the behavior of the child, others are more subtle and difficult to diagnose. For example, severe physical disability is readily apparent in the child's behavior, but a specific learning disability is much more difficult to identify. The teacher's task is to identify children who need to be referred for an intensive evaluation which will determine if they have a special handicapping condition.

SCREENING AND DIAGNOSIS

The first step in identification of handicapping conditions is the screening procedure. Developmental assessment of children in a center is primarily conducted to identify each child's developmental level and provide an individualized educational program. Under federal legislation and in most federally sponsored programs, early identification of special needs is a priority goal. All staff should be alerted to signals of handicapping conditions in preschool children. Routine developmental assessment will thus be an effective element in screening for handicapping conditions.

The second step in identifying a handicapping condition is the diagnostic evaluation. Once a handicapping condition is suspected as a result of the screening, the child may be referred to an appropriate specialist for an additional evaluation. The specialist will usually conduct intensive, in-depth analysis of the child's condition, determine if a special problem exists, and recommend treatment for the condition. The specialist may help the child's teacher develop the individualized educational program which accommodates the child's special need.

Parents, by law, must be involved in the process of referring the child for diagnostic evaluation. The Education of All Handicapped Children Act (Public Law 94-142) establishes the parent's rights to be involved in planning and implementing programs for children with special needs. The law states that parents must be notified if their child is singled out for special evaluation. Thus they must be informed any time that testing or evaluation is being done for their children that is not being done for every child in the program.

When conducting the developmental assessment of all children in a program, teachers are following a routine procedure, and parental notification is not required by law. If a child should be evaluated more thoroughly, however, teachers are required to notify the parents and get prior written consent for the action. Although not required by law, we recommend parental notification of plans to conduct a program-wide developmental assessment and have included a sample notification letter in Chapter Two.

Screening, then, is the general assessment of all children to determine if there are signs of special handicapping conditions. Screening is part of the routine assessment using the *H.N.C.A.F.*. Diagnostic evaluation is a more in-depth assessment following screening. It is normally done by referral to a specialist who determines the existence or extent of a handicapping condition. Program staff must be alert to the nature of the handicapping conditions of preschool age children, and the signals of their presence, to be able to make these referrals.

SIGNALS OF SPECIAL PROBLEMS

The following list highlights characteristics an observer should be particularly aware of when conducting the assessment. They are key indicators that the child may have a special difficulty. These behavioral characteristics appear in many categories and can alert the observer to more specific problems. All assessment observers should know this list thoroughly. Signals of special problems include:

— Inability to distinguish shapes, colors, and similar objects that other children the same age can do easily.
— Poor or limited speech and language development.
— Poor coordination and balance.
— Lack of response to people and situations.
— Inattention.
— Unusual body movements or posture.
— Excessively loud and boisterous behavior.
— Lack of energy.
— Excessive anger or irritability or low threshold for frustration.
— Withdrawal, or remaining alone for long periods.
— Difficulty following directions.
— Lack of common knowledge most other children have.
— Either excessive or greatly limited use of imagination.

Most of these behaviors are indicators that could reflect problems in several areas of the child's development. For example, the indicator "inattention," could signal a hearing problem, a vision problem, an emotional problem, or a learning problem. The task at screening is not to diagnose the problem, but to identify a child who might have a problem and place the child with an appropriate specialist for professional evaluation.

TYPES OF HANDICAPPING CONDITIONS

Thorough discussion of handicapping conditions is beyond the scope of this handbook. Teachers and aides should receive specific training on identification of handicapping conditions, and on programming for and working with children with special needs. The child development or special education department of a local university or college can provide information on where to receive this training. All public schools have a responsibility for training their own staff in working with special needs of children and could be helpful in locating or providing similar training for the preschool staff. Below is a list of disability areas and some indicator behaviors that might be observed while administering the *Humanics National Child Assessment Form*.

BLINDNESS OR VISUAL IMPAIRMENT: Child constantly avoids close work, is hesitant when moving about the room, is unable to distinguish colors or basic shapes, rubs eyes frequently, trips over things, moves eyes in a jerky or uncoordinated manner, frowns or has constant headaches.
DEAFNESS OR HEARING IMPAIRMENT: Child does not respond to sounds, does not socialize or communicate with others, shows poor or limited speech, must have things repeated, turns ear to speaker, appears inattentive, is excessively loud, may appear disturbed, has frequent earaches.
PHYSICAL HANDICAP: Child shows poor coordination, exhibits faulty eye-hand movement, has poorly devel-

oped fine and gross motor skills, stumbles or falls often, exhibits unusual body movements or posture, tires easily.

SPEECH HANDICAP: Child stutters frequently, substitutes sounds, lisps, strains to speak, shows irregular speech patterns, pronounces many words unclearly, repeats words often, uses pointing rather than speaking.

HEALTH OR DEVELOPMENTAL IMPAIRMENT: Child has history of illness, suffers seizures, has difficulty in breathing, tires easily, is excessively irritable or tense, experiences great or rapid variations in weight.

MENTAL RETARDATION: Child is slow to react, has difficulty in understanding and following directions, exhibits poor motor coordination, makes very limited use of imagination, has difficulty paying attention, is easily distracted.

SERIOUS EMOTIONAL DISTURBANCE: Child cries excessively, exhibits uncontrollable anger, is very timid or withdrawn, deliberately inflicts pain or injury on self, exhibits uncontrolled shaking or trembling, demonstrates unusual emotional reactions (laughs at sad situations, etc.), is inattentive and easily distracted, sits alone for long periods without any entertainment.

SPECIFIC LEARNING DISABILITY: Child is easily frustrated, has a short attention span, exhibits problems in language development, has trouble distinguishing between similar objects, has difficulty in following directions, cannot recognize or identify body parts, demonstrates poor eye-hand coordination.

ARE YOU LIKELY TO FIND A HANDICAPPED CHILD IN YOUR PROGRAM?

The incidence of children with special problems is difficult to predict and will vary with the population served. The number of children who have special problems not previously identified is even more likely to vary according to the prior health care practices of their families. If most children in a group have had continuing health care since birth, many special problems will have been identified, and, in fact, the parents may call the staff's attention to the child's special needs. When children have had less than consistent health care, there is a greater likelihood of undetected problems. In either case, the chances of discovering an unidentified problem are great enough to warrant attention to the behavior signals presented earlier.

Project Head Start systematically reports the number of handicapped children participating in its child development programs. Although the project is under a mandate to serve handicapped children (at least ten percent of the spaces available in Head Start must be reserved for handicapped children), review of the figures from this program are useful in considering the overall incidence of children with special problems.

Reports from Project Head Start show that twelve to fourteen percent of the children served are found to have special problems. While some of these children are referred to Head Start because of the program's service to handicapped children, many others are identified for the first time during the program-wide developmental assessment/screening process. Based on these figures, a program of say 100 children may include seven to twelve children with special needs. Administrators may use the following percentage figures to develop some "ballpark" estimates of the numbers of children with special needs you might expect to find in your program. Certainly these figures indicate the importance of all staff members' being aware of the problem signals and conducting a screening for these special problems as part of the developmental assessment.

TABLE I
ESTIMATE OF PERCENT OF CHILDREN SERVED WITH SPECIFIC HANDICAPPING CONDITIONS, BASED ON SUMMARY DATA FROM PROJECT HEAD START

Disability Area	Percent of Children Served Affected by the Condition
Blind or Visually Impaired	0.6%
Deaf or Hearing Impaired	0.6%
Physically Handicapped	1.0%
Speech Impaired	6.6%
Health or Developmentally Impaired	2.0%
Mentally Retarded	0.9%
Severely Emotionally Disturbed	0.9%
Specific Learning Disabled	0.7%

A CAUTION FOR ASSESSMENT OBSERVERS

All children exhibit most of the behaviors listed on page 205 at one time or another, sometimes frequently, with no special need or problem at all. Most young children have speech problems, difficulty with coordination and balance, difficulty maintaining attention and the other characteristics described. These problem signal behaviors are seldom considered symptomatic when they occur in the general context of appropriate behaviors. These behaviors are normal and in some cases even desirable.

Your concern should be more with degree than the kind of behaviors exhibited. Only when these problem signal behaviors fall into a broader context of development or adaptive problems is there need for special concern. The assessment observers should consider if the problem signal behaviors (1) occur excessively in relation to other children the same age; (2) are used often in the place of more appropriate behaviors; and (3) interfere seriously with the child's ability to learn and to develop the more appropriate behaviors that help him relate to his age group. The observer must put the child's overall behavior in context and make a decision about whether special attention is warranted. At this time, someone else within a program, such as a specialist if available, should probably observe the child also.

In addition, parents are very helpful in understanding a child's behavior although you need to be especially considerate of parents' feelings. It is upsetting and frightening to parents for anyone to suggest that their child needs further evaluation. The more parents are involved in the overall assessment process, the more useful they will be in providing input into the decision made, and the more likely it is they will concur with the decisions.

THE LOCAL EDUCATION AGENCY AS A RESOURCE FOR THE PRESCHOOL PROGRAM

Under Public Law 94-142, The Education of All Handicapped Children Act, the Local Education Agency, usually a city or county school system, has increased responsibility for identifying preschool handicapped children. Whether a center is federally or state funded, a private day care operation, church-related center, of family day care home, the public schools will be interested in identifying what handicapped children are being served. In some instances, the public schools can provide special services to preschool handicapped children through their allocation of federal funds for handicapped services.

Each Local Education Agency has a person assigned responsibility for special education. He or she may be a full-time special education director or a part-time coordinator in the Local Education services. The special education coordinator in the Local Education Agency can be an excellent resource of both sources of training for staff and sources of service for children with special needs. This person can help teachers understand more about the federal laws that affect services to handicapped children and may be eager to talk about identifying children being served in a preschool.

PLANNING THE PROGRAM FOR THE HANDICAPPED CHILD

Program planning for the preschool child with special needs is based on the same principle used for all children — identifying where the child is developmentally and providing experiences to enhance her growth. Most authorities feel it best if the child can participate in regular daily activities with all children as much as possible. Specialists may help develop the individualized education program for the handicapped child. Special treatment, therapy, or programming may be required. Often the child's regular teacher will have special learning activities and objectives tailored to the child's special needs. The sample IEP presented in this chapter includes space to record special services and other information related to special education.

COMPOSING AN INDIVIDUALIZED EDUCATIONAL PROGRAM

An IEP organized the assessment results into the following components:

1. **What Child Can Do.** This is a statement of the child's educational performance in the areas of Social-Emotional, Language, Cognitive, Motor Skills, and Hygiene/Self-Help development. Administering the *H.N.C.A.F.* was your first step in determining what the child is able to do. Portions of the Child Development Summary Profile have been reproduced on the IEP to assist the teacher or parent in planning. This information serves as a quick reference in completing the rest of the IEP. Additional information, such as reports from parents and anecdotal records kept by the teacher, should be included to accurately characterize the child's skills in each area. The teacher or parent should feel free to attach additional sheets if there is not enough room for all necessary information.

2. **Annual Goals.** These are the areas of development to be emphasized during the school year. In order to insure the total development of each individual child, the five areas of development represented on the *H.N.C.A.F.* must be stressed for each child. Therefore, the long range educational goals will be concerned with Social-Emotional, Language, Cognitive, Motor Skills, and Hygiene/Self-Help development. While the Annual Goals will be the same for every child, the process involved in achieving these goals will depend on the results of each individual assessment.

Children's behaviors develop in the same sequence, but the timetable of their appearance varies according to the individual child. When he or she reviews the Child Development Summary Profile, the teacher or parent has a visual representation of the child's abilities. All developmental areas may be at similar growth points, or one or more areas may vary from the others. It may be helpful to identify the child's greatest strengths. Has the child stabilized more behaviors in one area than the others? This strong area may be used as a vehicle to promote growth in other areas.

For example, if a child's Motor Skill abilities supercede all other developmental areas, sensorimotor experiences using large and small muscles may be used to encourage progress in other developmental areas (Cognitive, Language, Social-Emotional, and Hygiene/Self-Help). A child's superior ability to control small muscles, for instance, may be used to provide successful opportunities for promoting feelings about self-worth: "I can string beads; therefore, I am an able and successful person."

Areas where the child displays the least developmental maturity may also be noted by viewing the Profile. If the child has exhibited considerably fewer stabilized behaviors in one developmental area than the others, this area should be identified as a priority goal in planning objectives for educational achievement. The teacher and parent can structure activities, tasks, and exercises to foster growth in this area.

3. **Instructional Objectives.** These are statements of short-term behavior expectations. Each annual goal previously listed is made up of various components. The teacher must determine in what area the child needs further development, and the instructional objectives then determine the purpose of lessons to be presented to the child. Sample objectives for each item appear on the item description pages in Chapters Three through Seven. These sample objectives are wide enough in scope to offer the teacher or parent the opportunity to use his or her special knowledge of the child's abilities and preferences.

In deciding where to begin selecting appropriate instructional objectives *in each developmental area*, the following guidelines should be helpful:

a. If you have recorded any items as having *occurred occasionally*, consider these first in planning your instructional objectives. Once a skill has appeared in the child's behavior, it is an indication that the desired ability is emerging. Therefore, choosing these items first when constructing objectives and planning activities will give you the opportunity to strengthen skills for which the child has displayed readiness.

b. If the child's Profile reveals only items which *Occur Consistently* in a particular area, go to the item immediately following the last stabilized item to develop the instructional objectives. You should choose two or three subsequent items to include in your planning.

c. If you find gaps in the child's Profile (i.e., items that are checked neither *Occurs Consistently* nor *Occurs Occasionally*) between circled items, include these gaps in planning your objectives *after* you have addressed any *Occurs Occasionally* items.

For each instructional objective, there are innumerable activities that can be presented to stimulate development. Several are offered for each item in Chapters Three through Seven of this handbook. Review the activities and determine which are most appropriate for the individual child. Each activity should reinforce the instructional objectives listed in the child's IEP. These activities do not have to be recorded on the IEP. Rather, they can be expanded in the lesson plans a teacher develops to guide her classroom activities.

4. **Monitoring the Child's Progress.** Here the teacher states how a child's gains will be evaluated. The criteria for mastery of the objectives and goals must be stated. For example, if an instructional objective relating to increasing the child's verbal skills is listed on an IEP, how will a teacher or parent determine the child's accomplishments in this area? Perhaps the evaluation of the child will require a period of listening to the child speak, or administration of a vocabulary test, etc. The instructional objectives on the IEP should be written in behavioral terms, so that the evaluation of progress can be seen easily. In addition, you should indicate the time when follow-up monitoring will occur.

5. **Educational Program.** Indicate the percent of time the child will participate in the regular educational program offered for all children. For a child not receiving special education, the percentage of time will be 100%. For a child receiving special education, the percentage of time would be 100% minus the percent of time in a special education program.

For children participating in a special education program, briefly describe the program. Indicate also any support services, such as special transportation, physical therapy, etc., the child will receive.

6. **Dates.** Indicate in this portion the time period covered by this IEP, including specifically the initiation and anticipated duration of any special education services.

7. **Signatures.** The persons participating in the development of the IEP (teacher, parent, medical or mental health, etc.) should also sign the completed form.

8. **Parent Involvement.** For special education programs, the parents' involvement in the develop-

ment of the IEP must be documented. Parents must be informed of their rights of "due process" and invited to be involved in the development of their child's IEP; also, they may agree or disagree with the IEP designed for their child. These practices are beneficial for use with all parents as well.

USING THE RESULTS OF THE H.N.C.A.F.: AN EXAMPLE

With the assessment complete, the task at hand is to translate the results into a meaningful educational program for the child. This portion of this chapter is devoted to presenting a complete step-by-step example of how to develop an Individualized Educational Program and how to select activities to use in daily lesson planning based on the results of the *H.N.C.A.F.* We fill follow the procedure for one child, Angela.

ANGELA'S H.N.C.A.F.

On pages 211-225 is a completed sample *H.N.C.A.F.* for Angela. The dates at the top of the assessment column represent the period of time that was designated for evaluation. As the items were checked, the date the notation was made was also included in the box.

Observations and comments pertaining to the developmental areas, with corresponding dates, have been included in the "NOTES" portion at the bottom of the assessment pages. The "NOTES" portion should also be used to record any relevant information obtained between assessment periods. For instance, if Angela were to draw a person complete with head, body, arms, and legs between the evaluation periods, it would be important to make a note to that effect. These notes should be read carefully before the subsequent assessment so all progress can be accurately recorded.

The results of Angela's *H.N.C.A.F.* have been recorded on the Child Development Summary Profile. The entries on the Profile form the basis upon which the Individualized Educational Program is developed. Please study the *H.N.C.A.F.* data presented for this child before you continue reading. Observe how the information is recorded and used in the Profile and the IEP.

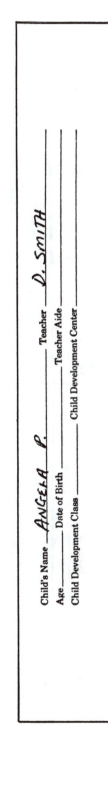

Child's Name __ANGELA P.__ Teacher __D. SMITH__

Age _____ Date of Birth _____ Teacher Aide _____

Child Development Class _____ Child Development Center _____

Humanics National
Child Assessment Form
Ages Three to Six

ABOUT THE FORM

The *Humanics National Child Assessment Form* is a checklist of skills and behaviors a child is likely to develop during the ages three to six years. Each item in the checklist is a sample of many related skills and behaviors and in that sense serves as an index of more general characteristics of development. Items in the Assessment Form are grouped into four scales that represent areas of child development: **Social-Emotional, Motor Skills, Language, Cognitive and Hygiene/Self-Help.**

Within each scale, the items are arranged in a developmental sequence, and space is provided for assessing the child four different times during the year. The Child Development Profile allows a visual representation of the child's ratings on each scale at the time of each assessment.

A NOTE TO THE PARENT

No one knows more about the development of your child than you do. This checklist is to structure some topics you and the teacher will discuss about your child. You may often want to add your own opinions and observations about your child's development. The information you and the teacher share is very important in designing an educational experience which will respond to and stimulate the individual nature and personality of your child.

DIRECTIONS

Complete all the items in the Assessment Form by observing the child in everyday play and work activities, or, if necessary, structuring special "testing" situations to let you observe the described behavior.

Score each item as follows:

Make No Check Mark —   If the characteristic is not present or the behavior does not occur.

Check in the "Occurs Occasionally" Column —   If the characteristic or behavior is sometimes present, but is not a consistent part of the behavior. The behavior has "occurred" occasionally but is not firmly mastered or developed.

Check in the "Occurs Consistently" Column —   If the characteristic or behavior has been adequately mastered and developed and occurs as a normal part of the child's behavior.

The *Humanics National Child Assessment Form* is designed to help the teacher observe the child in different areas of development and to follow changes over the years. It is not a normative instrument, which means it is not to be used to compare one child with another. It is to be used as a tool in planning educational and developmental experiences for the child, and is not designed for diagnostic or clinical evaluations. The form is intended to be used by teachers and parents to better understand and relate to the individual needs of the child.

©1982

HUMANICS LIMITED   1182 W. Peachtree St. • Atlanta, Georgia 30309
(404) 874-2176

SOCIAL-EMOTIONAL

Social-Emotional Expressing feelings and interacting with others. This includes, among other characteristics, expressing and controlling feelings, cooperating with others, showing social awareness, self-concept development, relationship to parents and relationship to adults in general.

		Date: 9/14 Occurs Occasionally	Occurs Consistently	Date: Occurs Occasionally	Occurs Consistently	Date: Occurs Occasionally	Occurs Consistently	Date: Occurs Occasionally	Occurs Consistently
1.	Identifies Body Parts	Points on request to face, arm, leg or foot.	✓						
2.	Shows Feelings	Smiles and shows other appropriate emotional responses.	✓						
3.	Separates from Parents	Separates from parent without reluctance.	✓						
4.	Relates to Adults	Calls by name two adults on staff; relates positively to adults but is not overly dependant.	✓						
5.	Interacts with Children	Talks comfortably with other children.	✓						
6.	Seeks New Experiences	Eager for and seeks out new activities and experiences; exhibits curiosity.							
7.	Maintains Interest	Maintains interest in play activity without encouragement from an adult.							
8.	Plays Cooperatively	Plays cooperatively in groups of three or four children.	✓						
9.	Modulates Voice	Controls volume of speech when directed and when participating in singing and language games.							

2

10.	Persists in Task	Stays actively involved in a chosen task until completed or for at least fifteen minutes.
11.	Shows Pride	Shows pride in accomplishments or products created; exhibits confidence in own ability to accomplish simple tasks.
12.	Shows Social Awareness	Shows awareness and respect for desires of other children.
13.	Protects Self	Stands up for own rights and does not permit other children to constantly take unfair advantage.
14.	Concerned About Fairness	Has a concern for fairness in what happens to other children.
15.	Demonstrates Responsibility	Takes responsibility for own behavior in staying within the rules of games and activities.
16.	Aware of Consequences	Behaves with an awareness of likely consequences of the behavior.
17.	Shows Creativity	Contributes original ideas and exhibits flexibility in play and creation of products.
18.	Exhibits Appropriate Values	Exhibits consideration for other, a sense of humor and self-discipline.

NOTES: Angela appears comfortable in the classroom. She needs to take responsibility in completing tasks and to take further initiative in play situations.

3

LANGUAGE

Language—Developing communication skills. This includes such skills as listening, following directions, memory, self-expression, and reading interest.

		Date 9/14		Date ___		Date ___		Date ___		Date ___	
		Occurs Occasionally	Occurs Consistently	Occurs Occasionally	Occurs Consistently	Occurs Occasionally	Occurs Consistently	Occurs Occasionally	Occurs Consistently	Occurs Occasionally	Occurs Consistently
19.	Follows Directions (I)	Follows a simple direction ("sit down," "jump," "clap hands," etc.)	✓								
20.	Extended Listening	Attends to a short story which is read directly, or played on tape or record.									
21.	Follows Directions (II)	Follows three or more successive directions in order.									
22.	Discriminates Between Words	Identifies similarity or difference between five pairs of words presented orally.									
23.	Labels Objects	Names objects in the environment.	✓								
24.	Speaks Informally	Speaks effectively in short conversations and in response to questions.									
25.	Initiates Conversation	Takes leadership role in beginning a conversation.									
26.	Speaks More Extensively	Holds a conversation, or shares a report, which lasts for one or two minutes.									
27.	Asks Questions	Asks questions appropriate to the situation.	✓								

4

#	Category	Description
28.	Uses Prepositions	Uses prepositions in describing relationships of one object to another.
29.	Uses Adjectives	Understands and uses adjectives and contrast words (opposites) correctly.
30.	Exhibits Auditory Memory	Repeats song or finger play from memory.
31.	Sequencing and Retelling	Retells a simple story in sequence.
32.	Exhibits Reading Interest	"Reads" a picture story book.
33.	Knows Reading Progression	Knows and exhibits the appropriate reading progression; i.e., from top to bottom of page and from left to right.
34.	Knows Alphabet	Recognizes and names the letters of the alphabet on sight.
35.	Uses Imagination	Can use imagination to create a simple story with some logical sequence.
36.	Plays Roles	Play activity involves pretending to be another recognizable person (e.g., I am a nurse, etc.)

NOTES: Angela needs a good deal of help in expressing herself verbally. She is reluctant to converse with other children in an instructional setting and lacks interest in prereading activities.

5

COGNITIVE

Cognitive — Acquiring and using information. This involves processes such as thinking, learning information, memory, imagination, problem solving and understanding.

		Date: 9/14		Date:		Date:		Date:		Date:	
		Occurs Occasionally	Occurs Consistently	Occurs Occasionally	Occurs Consistently	Occurs Occasionally	Occurs Consistently	Occurs Occasionally	Occurs Consistently	Occurs Occasionally	Occurs Consistently
37.	Visual Discrimination with Colors	Differentiates between four similarly shaped objects by noting their differences in color.	✓								
38.	Identifies Shapes	Identifies the following shapes: circle, square, rectangle, and triangle.									
39.	Classifies Objects (I)	Sorts objects into sets, matching objects according to color, shape, or size.									
40.	Understands Number Concepts (I)	Understands the number concept "one"; recognizes and names the numeral "1" on sight.									
41.	Knows the Five Senses	Can name the five senses and the sensory organ for each; e.g., "We hear with our ears. We see with our eyes."									
42.	Draws Person (I)	Draws human figure with head, body, arms and legs.									
43.	Compares Length	Selects longer of two sticks.	✓	✓							
44.	Compares Size	Selects biggest and smallest from four sizes of balls.									
45.	Understands Numbers (II)	Understands number concepts to five.									

6

✓							

46.	Detects a Pattern	Copies a pattern based on color, size or shape in stringing beads or stacking blocks.
47.	Understands Relative Qualities	Demonstrates understanding of relative qualities in such pairs of words as heavy and light, hot and cold, and fast and slow.
48.	Understands Number (III)	Understands number concepts to ten.
49.	Knows Seasons	Knows seasons of the year and how they relate to events (e.g., "School starts in Fall; Christmas comes in Winter.").
50.	Draws Person (II)	Draws human figure with details (fingers, toes, hands, ears, etc.).
51.	Classifies Objects (II)	Sorts objects into sets, matching them according to use.
52.	Recognize Fantasy	Can distinguish between fantasy and reality.
53.	Recognize Cause and Effect	Can recognize the causal effect of actions.
54.	Predicts Outcomes	Is able to predict the consequences of simple actions.

NOTES: _Angela needs a great deal of support and reinforcement in problem solving and concept formation on an independent level. Limitations in the cognitive area are paralleled by a similar lack of development in language development._

7

MOTOR SKILLS

Motor Skills — Using the body with control and efficiency. This consists of fine motor skills such as cutting with scissors or copying with a pen, and gross motor skills such as walking, balancing and jumping.

	Date: 9/14 Occurs Occasionally / Occurs Consistently	Date: _____ Occurs Occasionally / Occurs Consistently	Date: _____ Occurs Occasionally / Occurs Consistently	Date: _____ Occurs Occasionally / Occurs Consistently	Date: _____ Occurs Occasionally / Occurs Consistently
55. Walks on Tip Toes — Can walk on tip toes for four to five steps.	✓				
56. Walks Balance Board — Walks a balance board 6" wide, 3" off the ground.	✓				
57. Jumps from Stool — Jumps from 12" high object without falling.	✓				
58. Hops on One Foot — Hops on one foot at least three times in succession. (3 years).					
59. Catches Ball (I) — Catches bounced ball (12" diameter) in arms.					
60. Throws Ball — Throws three inch ball in generally intended direction.	✓				
61. Balances on One Foot — Balances on one foot for a slow count of three.	✓				
62. Works Puzzle (I) — Can put together a three-piece puzzle.					
63. Copies a Circle and a Cross — Copies a circle drawing a single line and returning to general point of beginning. Copies a cross.	✓				

8

	✓								

64. **Gallops** — Gallops continuously for a defined distance. (4 years).

65. **Dances** — Dances with sense of rhythm.

66. **Explores Space** — Explores space by moving in several directions.

67. **Works Puzzle (II)** — Can successfully assemble a simple five-piece puzzle.

68. **Uses Scissors** — Uses scissors smoothly and with moderate control.

69. **Copies Letters** — Copies large capital letters.

70. **Skips** — Skips continuously for a defined distance. (5 to 6 years).

71. **Catches Ball (II)** — Catches 3" to 4" thrown ball just using hands.

72. **Walks Backwards** — Can walk backwards in a defined space without bumping others.

NOTES: *Angela is performing satisfactorily in this area of development. Attention to fine motor activities is needed.*

9

HYGIENE/SELF-HELP

!Hygiene and Caring for personal needs in healthy ways. This includes recog-
!Self-Help –   nizing needs, accepting responsibility for satisfying needs and
               being able to take care of self in generally safe and accepted ways.

		Date: 9/4 Occurs Occasionally	Occurs Consistently	Date: Occurs Occasionally	Occurs Consistently	Date: Occurs Occasionally	Occurs Consistently	Date: Occurs Occasionally	Occurs Consistently
73. Allows Sufficient Time for Toilet Needs	Alerts teacher of needs. Controls need until toilet is used.	✓							
74. Dresses Self (I)	Puts on basic clothing such as shirts, pants, and socks without adult supervision.								
75. Knows Identifying Information	Knows own first and last name, age and sex.								
76. Uses Spoon and Fork	Eats with spoon or fork according to the type of food served.	✓							
77. Puts Things Away	Helps put things away following direction.								
78. Cleans Spills	Cleans up spills with direction from teacher.	✓							
79. Plays Actively	Plays actively on the playground without the teacher's constant supervision.								
80. Manages Bathroom Facilities	Manages bathroom facilities according to conventional routine.								
81. Dresses Self (II)	Is able to manipulate buttons, zippers and other fasteners, and to tie shoes.								

10

82.	Helps Prepare for Activity	Helps set out project materials on table.				
83.	Cares for Toys	Takes care of toys and materials.				
84.	Cares for Possessions	Shows responsibility for personal possessions.				
85.	Tries New Food	Samples a "taste-test" of new food when it is served.	✓			
86.	Identifies Food	Classifies food belonging to the four basic food groups.				
87.	Demonstrates Judgment	Exhibits proper judgment and understands safety principles.				
88.	Recognizes Weather	Understands weather concepts, identifies play activities suitable for weather conditions, and dresses appropriately for the weather.				
89.	Understands Travel	Locates classroom in the morning; knows afternoon pick-up procedure.				
90.	Knows Address and Telephone Number	Knows home address or can tell where home is located; knows telephone number for home or responsible adult.				

NOTES: Angela needs help in many areas. Relationships between hygiene – self-help, cognitive and social-emotional areas are apparent. Varied experiences are needed and should be encouraged.

11

PLANNING: Use the information from individual items in the checklist and the Summary Profile Sheet to focus on the child's strength and readiness for new experiences. Items checked "Occurs Occasionally" in the checklist are clues to readiness for experiences related to that item. Use the Planning Sheets to record specific areas of focus and activities for the child.

FIRST ASSESSMENT ___9/14___

Strengths

① Social-emotional area — particularly interactions with adults and to a lesser extent with children.

② Good development of large motor skills.

Needs Support

① Most language areas including prereading — need support.

② Concept formation and problem solving activities need reinforcement.

Follow-up Activities Planned

① Attend to behaviors that occur occasionally first — # 44, 46, 68, 85.

② Address all areas where assessment shows behaviors have not occurred.

SECOND ASSESSMENT _____

Areas of Demonstrated Improvement

Needs Support

Follow-up Activities Planned

12

THIRD ASSESSMENT

Areas of Demonstrated Improvement

Needs Support

Follow-up Activities Planned

FOURTH ASSESSMENT

Areas of Demonstrated Improvement

Needs Support

Follow-up Activities Planned

13

CHILD DEVELOPMENT SUMMARY PROFILE

INSTRUCTIONS: Circle each item checked "occurs consistently" in each sub-scale (Social-Emotional, Language, Cognitive, Motor Skills and Hygiene/Self-Help) using one color. Circle each item checked "occurs occasionally" in each sub-scale in another color on the chart below.

1st ASSESSMENT Date 9/14 Teacher D. SMITH

SOCIAL-EMOTIONAL	1	2	3	4	5	6	7	8	9	10	11	12	13	14	15	16	17	18
LANGUAGE	19	20	21	22	23	24	25	26	27	28	29	30	31	32	33	34	35	36
COGNITIVE	37	38	39	40	41	42	43	44	45	46	47	48	49	50	51	52	53	54
MOTOR SKILLS	55	56	57	58	59	60	61	62	63	64	65	66	67	68	69	70	71	72
HYGIENE/SELF-HELP	73	74	75	76	77	78	79	80	81	82	83	84	85	86	87	88	89	90

2nd ASSESSMENT Date ________ Teacher ________

SOCIAL-EMOTIONAL	1	2	3	4	5	6	7	8	9	10	11	12	13	14	15	16	17	18
LANGUAGE	19	20	21	22	23	24	25	26	27	28	29	30	31	32	33	34	35	36
COGNITIVE	37	38	39	40	41	42	43	44	45	46	47	48	49	50	51	52	53	54
MOTOR SKILLS	55	56	57	58	59	60	61	62	63	64	65	66	67	68	69	70	71	72
HYGIENE/SELF-HELP	73	74	75	76	77	78	79	80	81	82	83	84	85	86	87	88	89	90

3rd ASSESSMENT Date ________ Teacher ________

SOCIAL-EMOTIONAL	1	2	3	4	5	6	7	8	9	10	11	12	13	14	15	16	17	18
LANGUAGE	19	20	21	22	23	24	25	26	27	28	29	30	31	32	33	34	35	36
COGNITIVE	37	38	39	40	41	42	43	44	45	46	47	48	49	50	51	52	53	54
MOTOR SKILLS	55	56	57	58	59	60	61	62	63	64	65	66	67	68	69	70	71	72
HYGIENE/SELF-HELP	73	74	75	76	77	78	79	80	81	82	83	84	85	86	87	88	89	90

4th ASSESSMENT Date ________ Teacher ________

SOCIAL-EMOTIONAL	1	2	3	4	5	6	7	8	9	10	11	12	13	14	15	16	17	18
LANGUAGE	19	20	21	22	23	24	25	26	27	28	29	30	31	32	33	34	35	36
COGNITIVE	37	38	39	40	41	42	43	44	45	46	47	48	49	50	51	52	53	54
MOTOR SKILLS	55	56	57	58	59	60	61	62	63	64	65	66	67	68	69	70	71	72
HYGIENE/SELF-HELP	73	74	75	76	77	78	79	80	81	82	83	84	85	86	87	88	89	90

14

INDIVIDUALIZED EDUCATIONAL PROGRAM

Child's Name __ANGELA P.__ Date I.E.P Developed __9/14__

Person Responsible for Implementing __D. SMITH__ Projected Review Date __1/14__

Complete the individualized educational program based on **assessment**, observational and other information about the child. Circle appropriate item numbers below to indicate behavior that occurs *occasionally*, cross (x) numbers to indicate behavior that occurs consistently.

	What Child Can Do	Goals and Objectives	Monitoring Child's Progress: When and How
Social-Emotional	From the Assessment: X̶ X̶ X̶ 6 7 X̶ 9 10 11 12 13 14 15 16 17 18 From other observations:	Annual Goals: To develop social-emotional skills Instructional Objectives: To develop self-concept & social awareness	① Review all items not observed after one term ② Encourage further interaction and personal initiative in play situations
Language	From the Assessment: X̶ 20 21 22 X̶ 24 25 26 X̶ 28 29 30 31 32 33 34 35 36 From other observations:	Annual Goals: To develop language skills Instructional Objectives: To develop expressive language	① Observe child in activities requiring speech on a monthly basis ② Attempt to promote interest in words and books
Cognitive	From the Assessment: X̶ 38 39 40 41 42 X̶ ㊹ 45 ㊻ 47 48 49 50 51 52 53 54 From other observations:	Annual Goals: To develop cognitive processes Instructional Objectives: To promote problem-solving skills	① Plan work on concept development and pattern recognition. Review progress in 1 month ② Provide manipulative and concept-making activities
Motor Skills	From the Assessment: X̶ X̶ 58 59 X̶ X̶ 62 X̶ 64 65 66 ㊽ 69 70 71 72 From other observations:	Annual Goals: To develop motor skills Instructional Objectives: To develop fine motor skills	① Provide practice with scissors. Review progress in 1 month ② Plan fine motor activities over one term or more to reassessment
Hygiene/Self-Help	From the Assessment: X̶ 74 75 X̶ 77 79 80 81 82 83 84 ㊺ 86 87 88 89 90 From other observations:	Annual Goals: To develop hygiene/self-help skills Instructional Objectives: To encourage both hygiene and self-help	① Encourage food-tasting. Reassess after 1 month ② Support activities for concept development in this area needed

Educational Program

	Initiation Date	Ending Date
Percent Participation in Regular Education __100%__		
Special Education Program		
Other Support Services		

Plan Developed by __D. SMITH__ __TEACHER__ Parents participated in Meeting ☒ Yes ☐ No

__J. JONES__ __DIRECTOR__ Parents concur with I.E.P ☒ Yes ☐ No

Name / Title __Claudia P.__ Parent's Signature __9/14__ Date

© 1982 HUMANICS LIMITED / P.O. BOX 7447 / ATLANTA, GEORGIA 30309 FORM CD-506

ANGELA'S SOCIAL-EMOTIONAL DEVELOPMENT

What She Can Do

Angela has exhibited a number of behaviors that *occur consistently*. She appears to be well-settled in the classroom. However, she needs to become more aware of the social situation in the class, build relationships, take responsibility, and demonstrate increased self-concept.

Goals and Objectives

Attention should be paid to all missing items. Provide both structured and nonstructured environments to promote higher levels of social-emotional development.

Monitoring the Child's Progress

It may take as long as one school term for Angela to have enough experiences working with other children to make reassessment valuable. During this period, special attention must be paid to the building of relationships and the development of self-concept when engaging in formal and informal learning activities.

ANGELA'S LANGUAGE SKILLS

What She Can Do

Angela has made only modest beginnings in this area. While she follows directions, labels objects, and asks questions, she shows less proficiency in building conversations, using language, or becoming involved in prereading activities.

Goals and Objectives

There is a relationship between Angela's language development and her social-emotional development. She needs encouragement in becoming more verbal and in participating in activities which require speech.

Monitoring the Child's Progress

Angela appears to lack experiences in the use of language. Such experiences should be encouraged throughout the term. Reassessment should take place at the beginning of the next term.

ANGELA'S COGNITIVE GROWTH

What She Can Do

Angela's competencies in this area are quite limited at this time. She reflects behaviors which *occur consistently* in making simple comparisons and in discriminating between colors. Interest in size and patterns *occurs occasionally*. She needs work in concept development and problem solving. The relationships between language and thought must be developed. There appears to be a strong relationship between her limitations in language skills and her cognitive growth.

Goals and Objectives

Provide reinforcement in those behaviors that *occur occasionally*. Attention to size and patterns are immediate needs. Activities to develop concepts and build problem-solving skills should follow. Manipulative materials which deal with these issues will be important.

Monitoring the Child's Progress

The items which *occur occasionally* can be cross-checked after about four weeks. All other items should be reassessed after one school term.

ANGELA'S MOTOR SKILLS

What She Can Do

Angela has exhibited a number of behaviors in the motor area which *occur consistently*. Most of them can be categorized as *gross motor* activities. Her aptitude towards scissor-cutting has appeared.

Goals and Objectives

Immediate attention should be paid to scissor-cutting which *occurs occasionally* as a behavior. This should be followed by many experiences in the *fine motor* area.

Monitoring the Child's Progress

Readminister the assessment to check items which have not appeared after one term. The scissor-cutting activity may be reassessed after about a month.

ANGELA'S HYGIENE/SELF-HELP SKILLS

What She Can Do

Three behaviors *occur consistently* in this area. They deal with toilet needs, using a fork and spoon, and cleaning up spills. She has attempted new foods and so that behavior at least *occurs occasionally*.

Goals and Objectives

Reinforce the behavior of attempting new foods first. Note the relationships between behaviors that have not appeared in this section and related problems in the social-emotional and cognitive areas. A wide range of activities must be provided in this section.

Monitoring the Child's Progress

Reassess the food-tasting item after one month. All other behaviors should be checked after the first term.

SUMMARY

The *Humanics National Child Assessment Form* and this handbook* are presented for your use as tools in assessing the development of individual children and planning a meaningful educational experience. The suggestions in the manual are based on our own experience and are shared to aid you in using the instrument effectively.

As you work with children, you will personalize the way you use the instrument and handbook, and will add to the content new ideas and activities based on your experience. We hope you find the handbook relevant and flexible enough to adapt usefully to your own work with children.

DEVELOPING LOCAL NORMS FOR THE HUMANICS NATIONAL CHILD ASSESSMENT FORM

Utilizing Local Norms

Local norms are sometimes better and more appropriate than national norms. However, if local norms are based on a group of adequate size (usually 200 or more students), they can be used in most of the ways that national norms are used. Some possible uses of local norms include: (1) describing a student's standing with respect to the local group, (2) comparing the scores of two local students, (3) comparing a student's standing with his school and/or system standing, and in the case of the Humanics National Child Assessment Form comparing a student's scores with others who have made similar scores and have not been successful in first grade academic work.

The reader who is planning on developing local norms for the Humanics National Child Assessment Form would find it helpful to consult several sources on educational and psychological measurement and evaluation. For example, Thorndike and Hagen(1969) and Anastasi (1976) have excellent chapters on norms. An additional source on basic statistical concepts would also be helpful.

Collecting Data for Local Norms

Scores for 200 or more students are usually desirable for constructing local norms. Percentile ranks can be computed for a smaller group of students, but the larger the group, the more stable the norms will be. The Educational Testing Service(ETS) (1964) points out that the norms do not have to come from the same testing period and can be accumalated over a period of several years. The scores used, however, should all be obtained on comparable groups of students at comparable stages in their schooling. You would need a separate set of data, one for 3,4 year and 5 year olds and one for those entering first grades.

For those schools collecting data over several years it is recommended that they drop the oldest data from their local norms and add the newest data periodically. Systems doing this, may also want to keep a running record of the mean and variance of local norms as desribed by Elliot and Bretzing (1980), and if using a computer, by Krus and Ceurvorst (1978).

Making a Grouped Frequency Distribution

After acquiring a pool of test data, the initial step in constructing local norms is to prepare a frequency distribution.

1) Find the highest score and lowest score.

2) Set up two-score intervals running from the highest score down to the lowest.

3) List the score intervals from the highest to the lowest on a sheet of lined paper, such as legal pad. (See example in the first column of the table on the next page.)

4) Tally the number of students earning scores falling in each interval. (See table, second column.)

5) Sum the tallies in each score interval and record these frequencies in the third column, which is headed "Frequency."

Table 1

LOCAL NORMS SCORE DISTRIBUTION SHEET

Name of Test _____ Date of Testing _____

School(s) or system _____ Age _____

Selected Characteristics _____ boys; _____ girls; mean months in center-8.12 _____
of local Norms Group

Score Interval	Tally (consistently)	Frequency	Cumulative Frequency	Percentile Rank
Social Emotional				
1-3				
4-6				
7-9				
10-12				
13-15				
16-18				
Language				
19-21				
22-24				
25-27				
28-30				
31-33				
34-36				
Cognitive				
37-39				
40-42				
43-45				
46-48				
49-51				
52-54				
Motor Skills				
55-57				
58-60				
61-63				
64-66				
67-69				
70-72				
Hygiene/Self-Help				
73-75				
76-78				
79-81				
82-84				
85-87				
88-90				

Total Number of Students _____

Computing Percentile Ranks

Cumulative frequencies are obtained by adding frequencies in the score distributed from the bottom up. The number opposite each score interval equals the sum of the frequency for that interval and all frequencies below it. (See table, fourth column.) Percentile ranks for any score interval are computed from these cumulative frequencies in the following manner:

1) Find one half the frequency for a particular score interval,

2) Add the result of (1) to the cumulative frequency for the score interval just below the interval being computed,

3) Divide the result of (2) by the total number of students in the norms group, and

4) Multiply the answer from (3) by 100.

For the 60-61 score interval in the table, the following computations were made:

1) $1/2 \times 24 = 12$

2) $12 + 146 = 158$

3) $158 \div 218 = .72$ (taking the answer to the nearest hundredth)

4) $.72 \times 100 = 72$

The percentile rank of 72 is recorded in the fifth column of the table.

According to ETS (1964), percentile ranks computed in this manner are mid-percentile ranks, i.e., they correspond to the midpoint of the two-score interval and apply approximately to both scores in the interval.

In the computation of local norms utilizing larger score intervals, the following formula may be helpful:

$$PR = 100 \left[\frac{(\text{Raw score} - \text{LRL of class})}{i} \times (\text{f of the class}) + (\text{cum. f of the interval}) \right] \div N$$

Symbols:
- PR = Percentile Rank
- LRL = Lower Real Limits
- i = Number of units contained in the score interval
- f = Frequency
- N = Sum of the Frequencies (total cases)

Interpretation of Local Percentile Norms

Percentile rank is a statement of a person's relative position within a defined group.

Many test publishers, as well as developers of local norms, have found it useful to prepare norms tables in the form of percentile bands. The objective in using percentile bands is to keep the test user from attaching unwarranted precision to a test score. The band that is usually reported extends one standard error of measurement on either side of the obtained score. The reader, who is interested in setting up percentile bands for local norms on the Humanics National Child Assessment Form should consult any elementary or basic text on statistics in education and psychology for suggested procedures.

REFERENCES

Anastasi, A. (1982). *Psychological testing* (5th ed.). London: The MacMillan Company, Collier-MacMillan Limited.

Ausubel, D. P. (1959). Viewpoints from related disciplines: Human growth and development. *Teachers College Record, 60,* 245-254.

Bereiter, C. & Englemann, S. (1966). *Teaching disadvantaged children in the preschool.* New York: Prentice-Hall.

Blair, G. M. & Jones, R. S. (1960). Readiness. In C. W. Harris (Ed.), *Encyclopedia of educational research* (3rd ed.). Toronto, Canada: The MacMillan Company.

Bolig, J. R. & Fletcher, G. O. (1973). The MRT vs. ratings of kindergarten teachers as predictors of success in first grade. *Educational Leadership, 30,* 637-640.

Brandt, R. M. (1971). The readiness issue today. In D. Hold and H. Kicklighter (Eds.), *Psychological services in the schools: Reading in preparation, organization and practice.* Dubuque, Iowa: Wm. C. Brown Company, Publishers.

Brenner, A. (1967). Re-examining readiness. *Childhood Education, 43,* 453-457.

Chew, A. L. (1977). *The design, development, and validation of an individually administered school readiness test.* Unpublished doctoral dissertation, The University of Mississippi.

Chew, A. L. (1981). *The Lollipop Test: A Diagnostic Screening Test of School Readiness.* Atlanta, GA: Humanics Limited.

Chew, A. L. (1983, November). *Validation of an individually administered school readiness test.* Paper presented at the Georgia Educational Research Association Meeting, Athens, GA.

Chew, A. L. (1985, November). *Investigation of the Lollipop Test as a pre-kindergarten screening instrument.* Paper presented at the Georgia Educational Research Association Meeting, Atlanta, GA.

Chew, A. L., Kesler, E. B., & Sudduth, D. H. (1984). A practical example of how to establish local norms. *The Reading Teacher, 38,* 160-163.

Chew, A. L., & Morris, J. D. (1984). Validation of the Lollipop Test: A Diagnostic Screening Test of School Readiness. *Educational and Psychological Measurement, 44,* 987-991.

Chew, A. L. & Morris, J. D. (1987). Investigation of the Lollipop Test as a pre-kindergarten screening instrument. *Educational and Psychological Measurement, 47,* 467-471

Construction and using local norms. (1964). Princeton, N.J.: Education Testing Services.

Ferguson, G. A. (1971). *Statistical analysis in psychology and education* (3rd ed.). New York: McGraw-Hill Book Company.

Krus, D. J. and Ceurvorst, R. W. (1978). Computer assisted construction of variable norms. *Educational and Psychological Measurement, 38,* 815-18.

Kulberg, J. M. & Gershman, E. S. (1973). School readiness: Studies of assessment procedures and comparison

Nic, N. H. & others. (1970). *Statistical package for the social sciences* (2nd.). New York: McGraw-Hill Book Company.

Silberberg, M., Silberberg, M., and Iverson, I. (1972). The effects of kindergarten instruction in alphabet and numbers on the first reading. *Journal of Learning Diabilities, 5,* 254-261.

Telegdy, G. A. (1975). The effectiveness of four readiness tests as predictors of first grade academic achievement. *Psychology in the Schools, 12,* 4-11.